MAKING WAVES

CREATING RIPPLE EFFECTS
THAT CAN CHANGE THE WORLD

PRODUCED BY Terri Levine, PhD

Edited by Lil Barcaski and Linda Hinkle

Published by: GWN Publishing
www.GWNPublishing.com

Cover Design: Kristina Conatser Captured by KC Designs

ISBN: 979-8-9867817-4-7

I dedicate this book to YOU! Why? You are the one who makes the ripples that lead to the waves that make a difference for humanity. I want you to know that YOU create great influence in the lives of others, and you are creating impact, influence, and your legacy as you serve the greater good.

We are all indebted to YOU for being who you are.

Keep creating ripples. I celebrate YOU and thank you for being YOU!

Connect with our like-minded community of conscious leaders doing business heart-to-heart.

TERRI LEVINE

CONTENTS

TERRI LEVINE

INTRODUCTION

by Terri Levine

You picked up this book because the title intrigued you or you know one or some of the authors.

Before you begin reading, I want to ask if you ever found yourself in the trap of thinking you have to make a difference all by yourself.

We designed and created this book because we believe it is important to remember that you have a lot of power and influence and you can make a difference. It is just a matter of knowing what to do. You can transform the world.

Humans are driven by our desire to see change. I believe you decided to read this book because you want to BE the change. You want to be the solution. You see the world and the problems in front of you and you desire to make positive transformations.

As you read each chapter, I encourage you to be an innovator.

> *"I alone cannot change the world, but I can cast a stone across the water to create many ripples."*
> —MOTHER TERESA

When I was a child, I always thought that skipping stones across a lake would be the best way to make a path on the water. However, as I grew up, I began to realize that it was the waves of the water that created ripples. In the same way, if you were to let go of a stone it would create waves along the way.

One day I dropped a rock into a lake and saw that the lake ripples were much larger than the rock itself. This is exactly what we are going to share with you in this book, so you can make bigger ripples, and together we can make waves.

Have you ever felt a ripple? I think you have. You may not have noticed it at the time, yet it has made an impression on you. Life is filled with ripples if we are paying attention.

THE STONE IS YOU!

You are the stone that creates the ripples. You can be a rock and make bigger ripples or you can be the stone and join others who have stones and watch the waves grow.

There is no such thing as "one, tiny step." There are, however, many small actions that can make a big difference. If you want to make a difference in the world, think about what you can do now.

Take for example the act of kindness which can have far-reaching effects. It may be an understatement to say that a person's mood can affect the entire family. You can control your mood. The kindness you show towards others will be returned to you.

You will receive far more kindness and appreciation in return for your kindness than you could ever imagine. Kindness is always a choice.

Let's see how this works in the world. You see someone throw trash on the sidewalk where you and your friend are walking. You take the time to clean up their trash. Your friend sees you do that and then they start doing the same in their neighborhood based on what you modeled.

Or, maybe you chose to volunteer for a non-profit. Your children see how you contribute. They decide to follow suit and start a lemonade stand and want to donate the proceeds to charity.

In both cases, you were the catalyst for others to take action. You have created the ripple.

You never know how far your ripple will go, yet know that your ripple will go far. You could change the destiny of a troubled family, or you could create a new work ethic or pride in people. You could even change the destiny of the world. It all depends on how you respond to what you see and what you know. Your actions will always have consequences, and the ripple effect will always be real.

You are in control of the kind of ripples you make. You can make a positive ripple that will have a positive impact on your life and the lives of others. On the other hand, you can make a ripple that will have a negative impact.

MAKE A DIFFERENCE WITH POSITIVE RIPPLES

> *"You should be the change you want to see
> in the world."*
> —GANDHI

In this book, you will see how the authors are creating positive ripples to help companies grow, create health and well-being, enhance communication, develop better relationships and so much more.

Instead of worrying about how you are going to make a difference in the world and making the impact you want and dream of and feeling dispirited and disheartened, you will learn how to make positive ripples and be able to transform more lives and see how big your ripple can be.

If you have a problem that you want to solve, do it now.

RIPPLES CREATE WAVES

A ripple effect is one of the best ways to make a positive impact on the world. This can be done in many ways, some simple being; donating to charity, starting a social group, creating a project, starting a company, or even just volunteering. There are many ways to make a positive impact on the world.

I ask you to give some thought to how you want to make a difference as you get inspiration from these transformational authors and journal what those ways might be.

Imagine what you would feel if you started a company whose mission is close to yours and you have the ability to create endless ripples.

It is my belief that people need to contribute to have a meaning-ful life. Nobody is perfect and everyone is pushed to do more, be more. You cannot ignore the force that keeps you awake at night and pushes you to do more and to be more.

When you start making an impact and doing things that make a difference, in my experience, you will feel:

- Strong and powerful
- Grateful
- Fulfilled
- Successful
- Happy
- Passionate

This book teaches you to how to create and expand your ripple effect as you vicariously peer into the lives of the authors who share transparently and give you tips and tools, too.

When you are trying to influence people, it is important to know to be mindful of your own actions and words. People must be able to see your intentions and the positive changes that you are making. Our authors, by contributing their chap-ters in this book, are here to inspire you to create your own ripple effect. Remember, when you make small changes, you are able to make a big difference.

5 WAYS TO CREATE YOUR RIPPLE EFFECT

Don't complain you haven't done it yesterday. Don't promise yourself you will start tomorrow. Start now! Start today!

1. IDENTIFY YOUR MOST IMPORTANT PRIORITIES

If you are a little unsure of what your life mission is, take time to identify it. However, just starting with a single mission will not help you to find out what you care about, so you need to be aware of what you care about, to find out what you should be doing with your life.

2. SHARE THIS MISSION WITH YOUR FRIENDS

The best way to spread information is by writing or talking about it to others. So, once you identify your mission, start spreading the news. It doesn't matter if you are not an expert at writing, speaking, or creating videos - it is all about caring. Start by writing a short post or doing a short video on the topic you love. Send this to your friends and share it on social media.

3. TALK ABOUT YOUR LIFE WITH SOMEONE

Talking to a supportive person can help you to form your own ideas on how to have the impact you want to have. And you can inspire the other person to do the same. And you can also be friends and talk periodically about what you are going to do and keep each other accountable.

4. HELP SOMEBODY YOU CARE ABOUT

You don't have to change your entire life in a day. You can change someone else's life. Helping others is the best way to stop feeling helpless. Whom are you going to help today?

5. STAY INSPIRED!

Inspiration can come from many places. It is often from seeing other people doing things we dream of doing. When we are inspired, we can inspire others, as we are all connected. This book is an inspirational book to share and recommend to others.

Inspiration can come from a variety of sources, including books, videos of motivational speakers, talking to others, meditation, and visualization.

It's time to get down to the nitty-gritty and make some changes. Choose one of the 5 elements of change listed above and implement it today.

Now, enjoy the chapters from these amazing authors who are all experts in transformation and creating ripples, and making waves. Then begin making your own ripples based on your values, talents, passions, and life mission.

JOHN SEDEJ

I dedicate this chapter to my wife, family, friends, mentors, and coaches who poured their knowledge, experience, and love into me over the years so that I could become the servant leader I am today.

CREATE YOUR OWN LIFE OR SOMEONE ELSE WILL CREATE IT FOR YOU ... AND YOU MAY NOT LIKE IT

by John Sedej

We live in an amazing time. We can communicate with almost anyone in the world in a matter of seconds when vs. hours, days, or weeks not long ago. [Remember international letter posts with blue and red edges, home phones with a 20-foot cord, dial up internet?]

Access to information is more accessible than ever. Unlimited information (and opinions) is available in seconds that previously would've taken days or weeks to find, research, and verify, typically at a library. (Remember the Dewey Deci¬mal System?)

Yet, with all these amazing advancements allowing us to connect to virtually anything or anyone, a strange paradox has emerged. With this increased access, there has also been an increase in feelings of isolation, confusion, anxiety, and loneliness. This is especially true in larger urban environments like Chicago, where I live.

Another interesting phenomenon that emerged is how quickly people "believe" or "fol¬low" someone's viewpoint and opinions, and treat them as factual, merely after reading a few sentences on a tweet, post, email, or video clip. Rarely do people investigate the validity, accuracy of the information or the credibility of the source of the information.

If we were honest with ourselves, we take too many things at face value today, react when we should discuss, and believe "Facts" that are nothing more than opinions. We even find ourselves sometimes arguing over someone's unqualified opinion even though we know little about the topic or the person, but take a stand based on the "perceived stance" of the source of the information.

Why do we do that, do you think? Could it have something to do with an enhanced desire for constant validation and being "liked" (online and offline) or being "right" at the expense of some of our relationships and sense of community? Something to think about.

I bet that you, like me, have been the sender, receiver, questioner, and debater of the information discussed above.

This communication paradox is impacting people and business everywhere. We currently are emerging from a global pandemic that turned the world on its head. Business owners across the world found themselves having to navigate unprecedented economic, financial, health, and political challenges.

Some of these challenges mirrored those in the last downturn of 2008-2011, while others are entirely different. One thing is true, regardless of the cause of the struggle, more struggles are on the horizon, and you need to make sure to plan for it today, start creating margin in your life both with time and money, so when it inevitably hits again, you are better prepared to navigate through the storm.

I learned a lot of those lessons during the last economic downturn. In fact, those lessons were the catalyst for me starting the first iteration of my business, then called New Financial Path. Here is a little background so you can better understand where I was, what happened, what I learned, and how it led me to sharing this story with you today.

Let me take you back to late 2005. I had a growing and thriving mortgage business which is where I invested most of my time. I was offered occasional speaking, training, or consulting projects targeted to help small businesses and their teams grow in the areas of sales, marketing, leadership, performance, personal and professional financial management, and organizational health. I also was involved with my family's international marketing business, and then someone from church introduced me to a real estate investing group he was a part of, and shortly thereafter, I decided to launch a real estate investment company with a few new people I had met through this group. Shortly after starting the real estate investment business, it took off! We were lending, buying, rehabbing, and investing in lots of different types of real estate transactions. We owned several properties, some I knew about, some I didn't. [more on that later) and everything seemed to be moving up and to the right. We started taking bigger positions, took on bigger deals, leveraged more money, and became comfortable with this increased risk, primarily because of greed and the potential gains these opportunities seemed to offer. I placed way too much trust in those "partners", stopped tracking details as closely as I should have, the deals were not as rock solid as we thought, and you can guess where this is going. After a couple years, as fast as everything rose, it came crashing down even faster.

I went from having multiple profitable businesses and a seven-figure net worth, to almost the opposite in debt; practically overnight. This financial flip-flop was partially due the real estate fallout that began in 2008, and even more because of the poorly structured deals, high leverage, ridiculous financing terms, over-confidence, and as I found out, some fraudulent transactions my "partners" engaged in without my knowledge. It wasn't until everything started to fall apart that I started digging deeper into the details and asking questions I should have been asking all along.

What I uncovered was shocking to say the least, and the hole I found myself in was far larger and deeper than I could have imagined. There were multiple off the books transactions including properties owned, loans taken out, and commitments made by the other two partners that were upside down by high six-figures and growing by the day. They stopped responding to any calls, texts, or emails, and they disappeared. One fled to another country. I was scared, embarrassed, angry, frustrated, and freaking out not knowing how I would get out of this hole.

I was given lots of advice on how to proceed. Frequently that advice was to go bankrupt and walk away. I certainly considered it and it would have been the easiest option. The problem was, my name was tied to all these deals, and regardless of the fact that I did not know many of these deals even existed, I felt a responsibility to at least try to make this all right, or as right as I could.

I forgot to mention that when this all went down, the US government had just implemented wide-reaching legislation and regulations on the lending industry through the Dodd-Frank Act. Each state also had their own new regulations. As you can imagine, my real estate challenges messed with my ability to operate my mortgage business as well. Which by the way, was now my only real source of income.

So, against all odds and the advice given by most, I chose not to walk away and claim bankruptcy. Instead, I decided to take on all the debts, loans, mortgages, investors, etc. and try and figure out how to pay back and settle out everything and everyone and keep it from bleeding over into my mortgage business as much as possible.

Let's skip to the end of the story. Through God's grace, and a few miracles along the way, I was able to successfully get out from all the debt, never filed bankruptcy, never had a single property go into foreclosure, paid back every private investor their original investment, and some with interest. **It took over 6 years** with a ton of sleepless nights, negotiations, deal restructuring, occasional pleading, loads of humility, every penny I had to my name before the fallout, and hundreds of thousands more, and a redefined sense of values, needs, wants, and desires. I even threw a "BACK TO BROKE" party for me and my friends once I was "back in the black."

One huge blessing along the way that I feel was a reward for staying true to my values and of true integrity, was how the mortgage business continue to provide a fantastic revenue stream to help me live and continue to pay back all the investors, banks, etc., and ultimately the company completed a multi-seven figure sale a few years later.

One of the top mentors in my life, Jim Dornan, saw me outside the conference room at a hotel in Atlanta, acknowledged he has heard about my situation (still don't know how) and shared this thought with me that I cherish still to this day. He said, "I know it seems hard now, but you know you are blessed by this right?" I said, "Um, okay, I'll bite, why?" He said, "It's only money. That's the easiest one to fix." I had that second part on my wall and computer for years following.

I had many "AHA" moments over those years, and since, and can say that I was blessed to have that happen to me and it was one of the best times of my life. I am thankful for opportunity to build a new, more solid foundation in which to build a healthy, prosperous, and sustainable life. I redefined what I see as truly valuable and my faith grew tremendously. It sent me down a new path that equipped me to assist thousands of people and hundreds of companies across the world live a high-value life. Plus, it is indirectly the reason a girl from high school, that I had not seen in 20 years, reached out to me in late 2012 and became my wife almost a year later.

HOW DOES THIS APPLY TODAY?

Who knew that in a few years down the road, a global pandem¬ic would decimate the business world? Over the last few years, business leaders from around the world have been seeking us out to help them navigate these rough waters caused by the pandemic. In the last two and a half years alone, we have assisted hundreds of businesses leaders like you stabilize, adjust, pivot, and thrive once again.

It's worth mentioning that we brought aboard less than 10 percent of those businesses as clients. Not because we couldn't or because they did not want to work with us, quite the opposite. We believe in supporting those who need our help when we can help them, regardless of the financial gain. We know that sincere generosity always comes back around. This philosophy is proven by allowing us numerous opportunities so we can be selective in who we choose to work with.

I'd like to take a minute and walk you through a simple exercise that can help you measure your focus, identify your "WHY," and determine if your short term activities are aligned with your long-term goals. If you complete this exercise, I promise you will have more clarity, free time, confidence in your decision making, peace, a happier team, and make more money.

1. Why did you decide to start your business?

2. Is your business today what you expected to be at this point?

3. What is your main motivation for continuing to operate and run it today?

4. Do you have a well-defined exit strategy with a date, time, and exact financial metrics?

5. Who or what has the biggest influence on your business today?

6. If you could improve one thing in your business today, what would it be?

Here are a few more bonus questions for you to go deeper and gain even more clarity:

BONUS: REFLECTION QUESTIONS:

1. How would you define your ideal life?

2. With who and where are you spending your time each day?

3. On a scale of 1-10, how much does someone else's opinion or approval influence your daily decisions?

4. If that person were no longer a factor, how might you change your answers?

5. If you did not achieve these goals, how would you feel?

In the movie "*Wall Street: Money Never Sleeps*" Jacob Moore (Shia LaBeouf) asks Bretton James (Josh Brolin), "**What is your number?**"

Bretton answers, "**More.**"

That's definitely a dramatic Hollywood line, however, it rings true for many people today.

LaBeouf's character was trying to get an answer to a question that many fail to answer in their personal and business lives and wonder why they feel they haven't yet succeeded. That question is, "How Much is **Enough**?" (aka. What is Your Number?)

When you begin with the end in mind, clearly define what your ideal lifestyle and life looks like, and base it on what is most valuable to you, I can almost guarantee that it is less than you think.

Until you clearly define where you are going, you will never end up where you want to go. Instead you will value time, money, energy, and relationship currency with your family, friends, team, and clients running your race with a vaguely defined finish line.

As one of my mentors, Nancy Dornan says, *"If you don't know where you are going, you'll end up where you're headed."*

Remember this, on the other side of your "enough" is a life of increased generosity, opportunities, peace, significance, influence, and impact. You will be able to be more selective in the projects, clients, and opportunities that you engage in.

You can stop living the **"Rise and Grind"** life and start living the **"Get Up, Give, and Live"** life!

As a business leader, you must find time to plan, think, and be proactive. We all have things competing for our time and atten¬tion like: Employee demands, health challenges, the pull of the culture, sales and marketing plan adjustments, tech disrup¬tions, competition, vendor/supply chain issues, cost fluctua¬tions, personal and family demands, and the occasional global pandemic.

These can knock good leaders off kilter from time to time. However, great leaders find their true north quickly and get back on track faster than most other leaders. Find your True North!

To do that, you might need assistance from a consultant, coach, partner, counselor, agency, etc. To seek out and invest in the help you need is a sign of strength, not weakness.!

Be cautious on whom you take advice from. There is no shortage of people claiming to be an expert and willing to give or sell you advice, program, etc. Sorting out the fakes from the real deal isn't always easy or obvious. Finding someone like me that has proven results, offers guaranteed returns, and is willing to put their money where their mouth is, well, that is almost impossible... Until now.

Here are some steps you can take when you find yourself seeking assistance:

1. Always make sure you know WHY you are in business.

   - It is your benchmark or your True North in which to bounce your decisions by?
   - The clearer it is, the easier it is to say "yes, no, or not now."

2. Be consistent in your leadership*.

   - You will be able to hire better people and keep those you hired longer.
   - You will be more profitable.
   - Your expenses will be more consistent, manageable, and predictable.

- Your team will be equipped to make decisions without your constant input and involvement, freeing you up to be more strategic and less reactive.

Remember these TWO KEY POINTS:

1. A confused mind doesn't buy!
2. A confused team doesn't stay!

*REMEMBER: Inconsistent leadership creates less clarity and more confusion among your team, your clients, your prospects, your strategies, and leaves you susceptible to wasting time and money on the latest, fad, tactic, or gimmick.

> *"Everyone wins when the leader gets better!"*
>
> —CRAIG GROESCHEL

TIP: If you already have a qualified consultant, mentor, or advisor to run your decisions, do that BEFORE making big decisions. Their advice can help decide whether to say yes, no, or not now, and that alone could be worth 10X your investment with them.

FINAL QUESTIONS:

1. Would you like to gain clarity and focus only on activities that will get you to your end goals faster?
2. Would you like to have a roadmap that lays out the strategies you need to implement those results?

3   Do you have someone that is fully qualified to provide you #1 and #2 AND that you are able to be 100% transparent and open with?

If your answers are YES to one and two, and "no" or "not really" to #3, you might be the type of leader that would benefit from our proprietary *Business Breakthrough Review*™. If not, we can learn more about you and point you towards a qualified person to speak with.

Our proprietary *Business Breakthrough Review*™ shows well-established business leaders like you how to generate six figures of additional revenue **and** earn back six hours per week, in twelve months or less... guaranteed.

Does that sound like something you would be interested in for your business, with zero obligation or expectation to work with us afterwards? If yes, then go to this link below for information and to schedule your own, personalized, *Business Breakthrough Review*™.

We normally charge between $1500-$3000 for these reviews. However, **this is my gift to you** for purchasing our book.

CLICK HERE: https://roadmap.johnsedej.com

More money is always nice, but more time and the control over it is priceless. Few ever achieve this opportunity. Let us help you become one of the few who do!

If you are not ready to grow your business by six figures or more right now, or have all the free time you desire, then let's at least stay connected in my private Facebook group where you can connect and collaborate with myself and other leaders on how to run a profitable business AND have a great life at the same time. You will be able to share business building tips and strategies with me and other leaders like yourself in my private Facebook group:

CLICK HERE: https://www.facebook.com/groups/break-throughstrategies

Here's to you having the ideal business and living the ideal life of your design! Let us know how we can help make that a reality for you.

John Sedej - CEO & Founder
New Path Business Advisors
WEBSITE: https://newpathbusinessadvisors.com
PHONE: (773) 868-4385
EMAIL: Info@newpathbusinessadvisors.com

John Sedej

DR. MARIETTE STEYN

This chapter is dedicated to my husband, Cobus, the ever-patient listener to all the ideas and concepts living in my head.

WHY DIETS DON'T WORK:
HOW TO ESCAPE THE DIET TRAP AND START LOSING WEIGHT TODAY

by Dr. Mariette Steyn

Why is it that so many smart busy women are unable to get back to their natural weight, even when they exercise, count points, or follow complicated food rules?

It might not be their fault.

If you are a woman who thinks that the answer to lasting weight loss is having to rely on willpower while feeling miserable and hungry all the time, you are not ALONE.

According to the New England Journal, at any given time, an astonishing 15-35% of all Americans are trying to lose weight. Experts tell us that as many as 80 to 95% of women will gain back the weight they've worked so hard to lose... and then some.

Why are they not successful?

Let me tell you "The tale of two women", both professionals in their 50's, that wanted my help to release unwanted weight.

They were remarkably similar. Both women are busy professionals and have been struggling with the same body changes associated with menopause. But there was a difference.

One of them, Sandy, was only looking for HOW to get rid of the unwanted pounds. She wanted a quick fix and just wanted to know WHAT to eat... aka another diet.

When it comes to starting yet another diet plan, many women who have been on the weight loss rollercoaster for years, follow the same formula: Look for a "new" diet on Facebook or ask Dr. Google (as the old ones "didn't work" or "stopped working"), download some apps to count calories or points, figure out what NOT to eat (most of the things you love, sadly), and then they gorge on the "last supper" before starting the new diet.

Sandy did that too. She was skeptical, and not convinced that I could help her without telling her a list of what to eat. Off she went to another miracle diet. She used willpower and kept it for a few weeks. Initially, she did great, even losing some pounds. Her hard work and sacrifices paid off.

But then she ran out of steam. Her willpower started to crumble and hunger kicked in. She started to think "just this one time" For sure, one chocolate bar, cookie, or cheesecake for dessert can not really hurt."

When that voice got louder and omnipresent, it came as no surprise to me that her willpower failed her and her cravings got the upper hand. She quit. Yet again, this diet "didn't work" for her. She was back to losing and regaining the same pounds all over.

My client Janet, on the other hand, did not expect miracles. She had given up on quick fixes and knew that another diet was not going to be the solution. Heck, she tried them all. She counted points, exercised, and restricted what she ate when she ate, and how much she ate while being left hungry and frustrated. She was tired of being obsessed with calories and thinking about food all the time. Janet was ready to get off the weight loss rollercoaster—she would rather lose 10 lbs and keep it off, than lose the same 20lbs over and over. This time she wanted lasting results.

Janet was open to exploring other approaches that were not solely relying on WHAT she eats. It hadn't worked before and she had nothing to lose this time, except for some pounds.

And once she changed how she was thinking about weight loss, the scale confirmed that she made the right decision.

THE DIFFERENCE THAT MAKES THE DIFFERENCE

What makes this kind of difference in a weight loss journey? It is not simply that one woman wanted to get results more than the other.

Both wanted it badly, both tried many options before, and both regained everything that they lost before. Might the difference have been that Janet recognized what she didn't know?

THE MISSING PIECES OF THE WEIGHT LOSS PUZZLE

Imagine weight loss as a jigsaw puzzle. Many women are only aware of two pieces: nutrition and exercise. This recommendation of simply eating less and exercising more has for years been touted by both the diet industry and health professionals as the main solution to lasting weight loss.

As Albert Einstein said: *"The definition of insanity is doing the same thing over and over again but expecting different results."*

If one wants different results, one needs to do weight loss differently. If you have been asking: "if I'm so smart, why can't I figure it out?", you are definitely not alone. Heck, many women who get an A+ in their professional lives end up with an F in the weight loss department.

You just might need a brand-new approach. One that focuses not on WHAT you eat, but WHY you overeat.

ARE YOU TOO STUCK IN THE DIET TRAP?

Sandy was definitely stuck in it. The Diet Trap is the perpetual cycle of **gaining weight**, followed by **guilt and shame**. That often leads to another attempt to lose weight by **restricting** what and how much one eats. It is unavoidable. You will likely develop food **cravings** and an **over-desire** for what you cannot eat. So, voila! We **quit** the diet and start overeating again.

We gain back all the weight that we have worked so hard to lose. And some more.

Does that sound familiar?

WHAT IS THE SOLUTION?

You see, getting back to one's natural weight can be easy. I too tried to solve overeating by changing WHAT I'm eating. Weight Watchers, Paleo, Vegan, Low Carb, The Zone Diet... name it and I have tried it.

When I discovered the root cause of WHY *I've been overeating* for years, it all changed.

I have been eating for many reasons other than hunger. Here is the thing: food only solves physical hunger. Have you ever ended up after dinner in front of the fridge looking for something to eat, even if you are not hungry at all? Next time that happens, ask yourself: "If I'm not hungry, why am I eating?"

Many of us are simply not aware of what I call our "hidden hunger." We eat because we are lonely, sad, stressed, bored, upset, procrastinating, and many more reasons.

Food can not solve "hidden hunger." Combine that with our over-desire for concentrated pleasure in the form of sugar and fat, and it all becomes much clearer. It reminds me of the Elvis song, "We're caught in a trap, I can't walk out, because I love you (sugar and fat) too much baby."

THE LASTING WEIGHT LOSS SOLUTION

Hi, I am Dr. Mariette Steyn, a weight loss and mindset transformation coach, physician, and entrepreneur.

I have been one of "those women" that have been on the weight loss rollercoaster for most of my adult life. I am no different from you. It was not until I looked deeper into the connection between appetite, self-control, and the brain that I was able to identify the missing pieces.

If SCIENCE tells us that the main reasons for struggling to lose weight and regaining it are ...

- food cravings
- emotional eating
- sabotaging thoughts
- feeling out of control around food

Why do we continue to focus solely ON WHAT WE EAT?

My medical training gave me only part of the answer. When I started studying the brain and behavior, it became clear what was missing. Diets are purely band-aids combined with the message of eating less and exercising more, and can seldom give women the lasting weight loss they desire.

HOW TO START LOSING WEIGHT TODAY AND KEEPING IT OFF

My approach is a simple 3-step solution.

1. DITCH THE DIETS. No complicated food rules, calorie counting, or lists. Get out of the diet trap.

2. FIND THE THOUGHTS driving your "hidden hunger" and overeating

3. DEVELOP BRAND NEW SKILLS to manage food cravings and sabotaging thoughts.

Weight loss is a journey. Instead of thinking about how "difficult" it is, think about how you can make weight loss easy with tiny changes. Just pick one new thing to try. Write it down. See what is working and what is not. If it works, do more of it. If it doesn't, try something different. Become the scientist and not the judge. Start right now. No gorging on a "last supper" or spending days on goal setting and planning.

Here are a few quick start ideas:

- ONLY EAT WHEN YOU ARE HUNGRY: Yip, ask yourself every time before you eat if you are hungry. If in doubt, drink a glass of water and wait 15 minutes. Then ask yourself the question again. Eat only when you feel physically hungry.

- STOP AT ENOUGH: Check in with yourself regularly when eating and ask yourself if you might be satisfied. (This one takes some practice!) If in doubt, wait 15 minutes.

- DITCH THE PERFECTIONISM: Of course, you are going to think you are not doing it right. Let go of all the rules you have for yourself. Good enough is good enough.

- **PLAN AHEAD:** If you want to uplevel, spend no more than a few minutes either the morning of, or the previous evening and write down what you **want to eat** for the day. Not what you think you should be eating, but what you like eating. Then just eat what is on your plan.

- **ASSESS YOUR PROGRESS AT THE END OF THE DAY:** Take a few moments to check in with yourself to see what worked and what you can do better tomorrow.

Sounds too easy? I promise you your brain will throw up all kinds of thoughts. If you have creme brulee on your plan, your brain will want cheesecake. Tacos? Your brain will scream fajitas.

My superpower is to help you nail down the thoughts leading to your overeating and then teach you simple, effective tools to manage your thoughts and move you forward, one step at a time.

Is it a quick fix? No. Does it lead to lasting results creating a new "forever" weight loss lifestyle? My clients say "Yes" over and over.

What is your next best step to start making the waves that create the ripples of lasting weight loss?

Want to move forward? Meet me on my website
www.rethinkyourweight.com.
I have a link for a free Masterclass waiting for you there.

It will change forever how you think about weight loss. One pound at a time.

> *"The best diet is the one diet you can follow for the rest of your life."*

JULIE MUSIAL

*I dedicate my chapter to my father who told me when
I was a child that I could be anything I wanted to be
as long as I was willing to work for it. His wisdom
and grit did not go unnoticed.*

HOW I KNOW YOU'LL CRASH AND BURN IF YOU CHOOSE TO RUN YOUR BUSINESS ALONE

by Julie Musial

The first business I started was called JAM Advertising which began in 2003. JAM Advertising was a media buying service for small business owners. I also provided marketing coaching and consulting.

JAM advertising had fair results considering the small amount of effort I put into looking for new prospects and self-promotion. The one thing I did for self-promotion was to publish my first book, *Advertising Evolution*. Back then I was making about $60,000 a year and had little overhead. Things were going along smoothly until 2008 when that little thing called the internet began to skyrocket.

It had been brewing for quite a while fragmenting the original channels of offline marketing (television, radio, newspaper, magazines, etc.) That same year the U.S. faced one of the biggest economic crises in my lifetime.

Suddenly, large advertising agencies were losing clients and scrambling to pick up any clients they could find, including smaller clients, like the ones I served. One day, in late 2008, my largest client told me they would only continue to retain me if I cut my prices in half because they could get the same service elsewhere for less due to the recession. I had become a commodity without differentiation. I walked on the deal and never looked back.

I realized at that point, that I needed to rebrand myself as different from other similar agencies. Instead of being a commodity, I became a digital strategist and a master's certified business coach. Neither was a small feat.

Business coaching was exciting and new, but a lot of it, for me, was in theory only because up until that point I hadn't run a company with sound business practices. I worked with hundreds of different business owners helping them to see what they couldn't see for themselves. I received all kinds of accolades from clients on how much I helped them increase revenue and reach their goals. The whole time I felt like a fraud because I wasn't putting into practice in my own business what I was teaching.

When I started Musial Marketing in 2011, I was excited! It was my new, shiny Penney. Yes, I admit it, I'm a serial entrepreneur. This was my third small business. I studied guru after guru on the West Coast and read everything I could find to learn the art of digital marketing. The travel and time commitment were expensive because I'm from Wisconsin. I hired many coaches, however, none of them were teaching business coaching and consulting. They were all boutique coaches specializing in things like signature talks, launching campaigns, motivation, building online technology, marketing, writing, social media, etc. I never did the math, but I'm quite sure I spent more than six figures on boutique coaching.

By that time, I was a content creation machine. By 2015, I had written and published my second book which became a #1 best seller; *7 Steps to Selling Your Work Online – Entrepreneurs Guide to Financial Freedom*. I also created an online membership site with 13 courses, launched seven webinars, and wrote well over 1000 blog posts.

You would think by this point I would have learned something from my past business mistakes. Instead, I ran Musial Marketing myself using contractors from all over the world with only fair results. I plateaued at about $60,000 while working a lot of hours. I also had a lot of expenses.

I finally realized, after toiling away for years and running myself ragged, that **the definition of insanity is to continue to do the same thing and expect different results**. I seemed to be doing a lot of things right with moderate success, but nothing was clicking.

I finally hired a business consultant/coach. I paid her $1,500 a month to teach me how to work "ON" my business instead of just "IN" it. She taught me how to plan, price, sell, market, automate, and systematize my business. Within five months of hiring my business coach, I went from selling $2,500 website jobs to a fully automated system where my next two clients bought $50,000 packages each! I was doing the happy dance and this trend continued. The $50,000 packages were for the same thing I was charging $3,000 for before hiring my business coach/consultant. The difference was in the marketing, product pricing suite, and sales presentation, along with systematizing, and automating my processes.

Right about that time, I realized how much my parents needed me. My dad could barely walk and my mom's dementia had gotten much worse. There wasn't any other option other than for me to care for them. For those of you who have never dealt with the situation of your parents or someone needing a big chunk of your time for their care, it puts stress on you that pulls at you emotionally and physically. I was already burnt out from the years I struggled in business.

I made a choice that just after I had made more money than ever before in business ownership, I was going to close my business to take care of my family. I was exhausted from the years I spent trying to build my business into a success without the right kind of help I needed. My parents have now passed on and I don't regret my decision even a little bit. Once I closed my business, I mourned the loss of it as if someone else had died. Deep down inside, I think a part of me died. I had a feeling that someday I would reopen my business doors with all the knowledge I had gained.

If I had to look back over the years, my biggest mistake was not hiring a business coach/consultant much sooner. All the money I spent on boutique coaches and travel was way more expensive than what I would have spent on a business coach/consultant. It would have saved me time, money, and exhaustion, not to mention how much more money I could have made.

Five months after both my mom and dad passed, I saw something on the internet which said, "Don't Get to the End of Your Life and Have Regrets!" My regret would have been not running a profitable business for a **significant length of time**. The rest is history and Musial Coaching and Consulting was born. https://musialconsultinggroup.com

Only this time I knew I had to hire the right coach/consultant from the start. I now know that every business owner needs a business coach/consultant to keep them from getting stuck and burning out. You need to surround yourself with people who have done things that you haven't done. Learn from their mistakes and not your own. Think about it, if business ownership was that easy, everyone would be a millionaire. And don't get me started on all the fake gurus on the internet whom I see constantly telling me about their process to make you an instant millionaire. I say, run. There are no quick fixes with silver bullets.

If you're going to run a successful business, you can't play small. You can't hold onto the security of what you have now in hopes of jumping to the other side. If you believe in your product or service, get off the trapeze and take a risk. Hire a coach/consultant. If you don't believe in your product or service, close your doors.

THE MOST IMPORTANT THINGS YOU SHOULD LOOK FOR IN YOUR COACH/CONSULTANT ARE:

- Are they someone that you resonate with?
- Experience: Do they have a proven track record?
- Are they, not commodity priced?
- Will they best suit your needs and not just try to become a friend?
- Are they timid or brutally honest?
- How long have they been coaching/consulting clients like you?
- What industries have they helped?
- Can they provide testimonials?
- Are they a coach, consultant, or both?
- Have they worked with people in your industry or similar industries and been successful in helping those clients?

There is a difference between a coach, a mentor, and a consultant. A practitioner can be one or all three.

COACHES facilitate their client's self-discovery through the power of listening and asking questions.

CONSULTANTS are diagnosticians, analyzers, and assessors, and give recommendations, solutions, strategies, and plans based on their training and experience.

MENTORSHIP is a personal development relationship with a more experienced person helping to guide a less knowledgeable person.

After having made mistakes for years in multiple businesses and finally hiring a business consultant to help me figure it all out, I have a burning desire to help people not make the same mistakes I made.

Today, I teach entrepreneurs and agencies who provide digital marketing services how to generate more money using my proprietary *"Growth For Digital Marketers Accelerator"* method guaranteed.

Download my Consumer Awareness Guide *"Five Deadly Mistakes on Why You Can't Find Prospects."* Go to:

https://howtogrowindigitalmarketing.com/

In this fact-filled booklet, you'll have your most burning questions answered on getting a lot of leads that want to hire you, and most importantly you'll know your next steps to ensure you overcome not making the money you want and finally achieve business success.

Julie Musial

ADITYA NOWOTNY

Dedicated to You, the seeker, realizer and manifester of true inner and outer abundance and to all the members of my "Team ENJOY"

INNER AND OUTER ABUNDANCE

by Aditya Nowotny

I am Aditya Nowotny from Salzburg, Austria. Over the past 35 years, I have taught more than 135.000 people on five continents how to meditate. And in the past ten years, I have trained more than 70,000 people in the field of network marketing, with nearly 3,000 business clients.

Being the son of a corporate man—my father worked for the Ford Motor Company on a Director's level—I soon decided, that being in the corporate system (which makes you a useful jigsaw piece but deprives you of who you really are) wasn't my destiny. I graduated college but decided to not finish my studies at Vienna Economic University. What I saw and experienced at this elite economical university was too limiting for my vision of life.

A J.O.B. and living in the hamster wheel till retirement, and then death, was never what I was looking for. I established that my goals were (and are) freedom, fulfillment, and abundance.

I started to meditate on my 19th birthday (still meditating to this day) to probe the inner depths of life and to experience the consciousness that goes beyond the physical world, a world I was escaping at this point in my life.

However, when I was in my twenties, my meditation teacher said something profound to me that would be a guiding principle for the rest of my life:

> *"I want you to become a millionaire both in the inner and in the outer world!"*

Mind the sequence: first, achieve true abundance inwardly, then become a millionaire in the outer world.

At the request of my meditation teacher I started teaching people meditation—first in Austria, then in the German-speaking countries, then all over Europe, and finally in the US, Brazil, Argentina, Russia, Ukraine, Nepal, Thailand, Singapore, Indonesia, Malaysia, and many other countries.

Having been a meditation teacher in over 300 cities worldwide, and meditating myself every day, I reached a pivotal point in 2009. More than 100,000 people had learned to meditate through my seminars and workshops, and most of these people were good-hearted, soulful seekers. But there was one element that was missing, many of them were having challenges in the material world and were often lacking money.

This reminded me of the words of my mentor: *"Become a millionaire both in the inner AND in the outer world!"*

I realized that my own gap was in the outer world. My task was to become a millionaire not just inwardly, but materially as well. However, I conveniently avoided the outer part of the equation. And according to that gap, I attracted people into my life who had the same gap.

If you choose to change something, you always have to start with yourself.

In 2009, I decided to become an entrepreneur and began to build a network marketing team. Then, in 2014, I started an information marketing business. By 2019, I had added coaching and consulting to my businesses.

My first goal was to 10x my monthly income. I went from $2,000 a month to $20,000 a month within three years. I did this by applying the Abundance principles.

I started to research all the secrets that lead to holistic abundance, "super-natural abundance", as one of my event organizers in Maui, Hawaii titled my teaching. A doorway, a portal, opened as I came to realize these principles and I started to teach heart-centered entrepreneurs, network marketers, and solopreneurs how to apply these principles in their own lives and businesses.

Outer abundance is a manifestation of your inner wealth, mindset, and goal-setting. When you come from a heart-centered space, when you are a mindful, spiritually conscious person, acquiring material wealth is quite often a challenge.

Conversely, materialistic people often suffer from an inner emptiness, sadness, frustration, and lack, as they have never cared for inner abundance in the form of light, love, peace, and bliss.

As the Yin-Yang symbol indicates, life is about both sides, the outer and the inner life, the material and the spiritual, to be the creator and master the material world and to be illumined in the inner world. A coin that is only minted on one side and blank on the other side does not carry any value...

Among my personal growth and business training programs are "The 30 Day Abundance Challenge", "Breakthrough: Awaken The Champion Within", "The 13 Golden Laws Of Mastering Money Energy", "The Flow

Challenge" and "The Ego Challenge" and I have served close to 3.000 clients with these courses as well as done personal coaching and consulting.

Here are some success stories:

AGNIESZKA DWORCZYNSKA from Krakow, Poland participated in my first Abundance Challenge in 2017. As a result, she more than tripled her income within three months and jumped two ranks in her network marketing organization.

What are her secrets?

Agnieszka is a good-hearted, loving, and wonderful person, who was first in a direct sales company where she was selling in the evenings, but not sustainably building a business. This all changed when she started a real community, a true family team with duplication.

This mindset change from selling to building and teaching, plus allowing herself to have the success she long deserved, provided the first step. Next were subconscious programmings and beliefs that the various steps of the Abundance Challenge transformed and upgraded.

Another important move was the reprogramming of family history and beliefs that show up in all of us reaching back as far as the last seven generations. We are all very much influenced by genetics and epigenetics and the techniques to upgrade these ancestral programmings lifted Agnieszka beyond.

She was, for the first time, not just earning an additional income with her business, but became able to live comfortably from her business.

FRANCIS HERDES from Heiligenhafen, Germany started out as a medical student but soon realized that the medical system and the stress of being a doctor were not meant for her. Francis started her own wellness and information marketing business.

Francis participated in numerous Abundance Challenges as well as in most of my programs and is a personal coaching client of mine.

According to Francis, her financial calibration—which some call the "financial thermostat"—changed decisively from just making do to having targeted amounts of money on her accounts and in cash.

The security from having more than enough (versus just making it) provided a tremendous change in her self-confidence and outlook on life. Having more than enough gave her the ease and security to really excel in her strengths, as opposed to always running behind.

Francis mastered the "triangle of wealth" that I teach:

1. how we receive money energy
2. how we keep money energy
3. how we increase and invest money energy

This is based on the principles of creation—preservation—transformation, that is inherent in the cosmos.

Francis also implemented a tip I gave her regarding recurring revenue and memberships which has become a strong pillar in her total income.

SUSANNE BECK from Seligenstadt, Germany is a yoga instructor, graphic designer, and network marketer of the purest ink. As you can see from this shortlist of activities, she was involved in a number of activities.

Susanne is one of the best inspirations and motivators of people that I personally know. She is hugely engaged and personally invested, but this lead her often to exhaustion. When she gave birth to her first son, this way of operating was not sustainable anymore.

In a personal coaching session, I advised Susanne to work only four days a week (in the first step five days) from the seven days she worked before our coaching session. Her natural reaction was," How is it possible to earn more and grow my business when I work less?"

This is a reaction that I often experience with my clients—before abundance consciousness sets in, many people are prone to two mistakes:

- They think the only way to earn more is to work more.

AND

- They set and keep their prices too low, not knowing the real value of their work.

In the economical crisis of the early 2020s, when many businesses experienced a downturn, Susanne and her team grew steadily and healthily. By doing less—working fewer days and less hours—Susanne learned to achieve more.

This is facilitated by the principles of **Time Abundance, Energy Abundance**, **Abundance in Action**, and **Abundance in Non-Action**, which the *30-Day Abundance Challenge* teaches and helps participants to implement.

Agnieszka, Francis, and Susanne are three wonderful people out of close to 3,000 participants in my programs, coaching, and consulting, who came from a heart-centered and inner abundance space and added true outer abundance to their lives in many areas. I am grateful that I have such wonderful client family members, and it all started with me making the change in my own life first.

How would YOU like to learn, assimilate and implement these principles of abundance in your life?

Go to https://adityanowotny.com/abundancesecrets to find gifts as well as access to the **Abundance Challenge**. To enjoy inner AND outer Abundance is your birthright!

DEE HAMPEL

This is dedicated to my nephews Chris and Kevin, whom I love to the moon and back. You can do more than you think; the power is inside you.

COMPLAINING ABOUT DOLLARS MAKES NO CENTS

by Dee Hampel

Do you complain about a 5% increase yet won't look for savings when buying?

This just absolutely does not make cents, don't you agree?

OMG, have you seen the price of gas? I don't know how I can afford to drive my car; if gas prices keep increasing, I will solely be working to pay for gas.

Talk about high prices. Each week I buy groceries, and it costs me another $50.00 for the same items. I may have to start selling body parts to pay for food.

Between Covid, logistics issues, and increasing prices, we don't expect things like this to happen in our instant society. But unfortunately, we were surprised; for some folks, it is just too much to bear. You can't control a pandemic, but you can control things like where and when to spend and what you do with your money.

I get where you're at and couldn't agree more! Inflation is at its highest it has been in our lifetime at a whopping 9.06% in just June alone in 2022. That is a total percentage higher than the previous month with no end in sight. Believe it or not, it has been worse! According to several sources, the highest inflation rate was in 1778 at a rate of ~30.19%, just two years after the founding of the United States. Talk about crazy. We are not at that point, and I want you to relax because there are thousands of ways to save money and spend less, and I am not talking about a bank account.

Being a corporate buyer for over 30 years where what I buy will make or break a profit margin and the daughter of a single mom who was a child of the depression, with a bit of creativity on how to look at things, makes for super saving skills and savvy. So don't worry; I will share some of these tools with you.

When people hear about cost saving, they think they have to spend hours wasting money and cutting coupons to save a nickle. I am not talking about clipping a coupon and putting a quarter in a piggy bank. Saving cash is mindset and know-how. Let's talk perspective. Yes, it would help if you had the right attitude. Let me explain. You have to have an open mind and be willing to put in a little extra work in the beginning, knowing where you are and where you need to be, and once you get the hang of it, it is super easy and fun.

First, you must know where to start, where you are number-wise, your assets and income, your expenses, and what is left over. So yes, this is where everyone must begin; if you are a small business, entrepreneur, going solo, or a household. Period! No, ifs and or buts. Then using those numbers, you will create a budget, which is the first piece of your savings puzzle. Knowing your numbers can be traumatic and an eye-opening experience. Yet very liberating!

Next, create a budget. Accounting software is unnecessary unless you are making high 6 or 7 figures; you don't need accounting software. This purchase is a mistake often made by entrepreneurs and small business owners, overspending on things they think they need. What you need is a little guidance from a CPA and a good grasp of your geographical area's local tax laws, which is about it. Budgeting can be as easy as a piece of paper, putting your total income as your starting balance, then your monthly expenses, and that is where you will start recording your ins and outs.

Take a detailed look at expenses. For example, what are your necessary costs, taxes, insurance, rent/mortgage, payroll, and utilities? Then, list your payments on a separate sheet and when they are due.

List absolutely everything you spend money on; if you have never done this, you can do this one of two ways. First, you can keep a money journal where you record every penny you spend and where you spend it. (I recommend this either way for both your business and personally). Or record what you spent last month analyzing all of your accounts, balances, and due dates. Then take your total of available cash in and subtract the funds spent. Is there money left over? Your journey begins now.

The next step is to review your expenses and see what you need and what is necessary! Don't forget those automatic credit card deductions, are they still used? If not, cancel them. Then, when the bill comes in, we pay it and don't look back. Trust me when I say this, you want to review monthly—credit card thieves and out and especially during challenging times. As a business, you also want to check your phone bills, looking for long-distance or fraudulent phone calls. Thieves are stealing phone numbers and ghosting them, and you, as a business owner, get charged if you are not careful.

Carefully review your expenses, and I can't say this enough. Expenses are your profit, vampires. They will steal all of your earnings if you are not watching the store. Based on my experience, these are a few other vampires to watch out for on desktop printers and ink; depending on what you print, use non-manufacturer ink. Finally, send your marketing materials to a print shop that handles smaller volumes; the price will be lower and more competitive. With a plugged-in cord, electricity still draws power; use a power strip and turn off the strip at night. Shop your electric supplier, and see if they will do an audit of your usage. They will tell give you ways to be more power efficient.

Barter or trade for services if what you provide can be a creative alternative. For example, if you have a big office with extra space, rent out an office or room for storage. Share trash services with a neighboring business.

Need extra labor? Check with local schools to see if they have any students studying in your field and hire an intern part-time.

Those are some basic tactics you can use. Another is to look at what you charge! For example, are you charging enough for your services or products? Not knowing the costs of your products is another huge mistake often made; tracking time and materials use, don't forget things like online meeting software, your cell phone, and internet fees. These are often overlooked depending on your business type and how you cost your product. You can either capture these costs by adding them into your pricing as a flat fee or as part of your overhead expenses. However, you want to include these costs in the products you sell.

Another way to look at what you charge is to work backward. For example, what do you want to make each month? Then based on your product pricing, this is how many new clients you need or products you need to sell.

A mistake often made by business owners and entrepreneurs is overspending on products and services you don't need. I know

I touched on this earlier, look for free versions of software or products that offer a trial period before you purchase. This step alone can save you thousands of dollars in your business lifetime.

So, let's recap what we have discussed. **First,** we created a budget and reviewed expenses; we determined what we needed and what we no longer used. **Next,** we made an aging so we know when bills are due and funds are needed. Then, we canceled and sold items we no longer required or used. **Next,** we have established less expensive alternatives to run our business and obtain services for less. **Then** we created extra income by utilizing extra space and hiring eager and cheaper labor. How to capture better product costing and reduce expenses, putting more money into our own pockets. **And how to save money.**

It has been my pleasure sharing these essential tips with you, and if what I shared with you today resonates and you would like more creative and money-saving ideas, you can follow me on Facebook at:

https://www.facebook.com/deehampelconsulting/.

DENNIS KEARNEY

This chapter is dedicated to my mother and grandmother for always supporting my ideas and aspirations, no matter how crazy they seemed.

CHOCOLATE TAUGHT ME ABOUT BUSINESS BUT FAILURE PREPARED ME FOR SUCCESS

by Dennis Kearney

PART 1

It's funny how we look back and wonder how the heck we made it through certain periods of our lives. It was no secret I began building my chocolate "empire" while working a full-time corporate job. Nor was there anything too extraordinary about this fact, as many people work multiple jobs, raise children, go to school while working full time—the list goes on. For me, that pesky day job not only paid my rent, car payment, and other bills—it also provided the funding to fuel my fledgling company.

Operating by the seat of my pants was pretty much the norm for me during much of my chocolate life. While this business method was often uncomfortable, it forced me to be creative and proficient in solving the endless stream of challenges that seemed to lurk around every corner. It was a bit like the paparazzi hiding in the bushes, waiting to pounce on their unsuspecting prey. Truth be told, the act of resolving the endless stream of challenges became somewhat of an addiction. Don't get me wrong, I hated the associated stress that accompanied many of these situations, but after conquering said challenge, I did feel good and dare I say, it provided a bit of a confidence boost. At least until the next challenge arose and my heart would sink again ever so slightly.

The honeymoon phase of my business lasted several years. The process of learning more and more about chocolate and building a business was intoxicating. And having prospective customers taste my product was downright ego-boosting. All they had to do was taste it and the deal was done. Who needed sales staff, the product sold itself!

However, they say hindsight is 20/20 and this was true for me. With all of my newly discovered business acumen, along with the daily duties associated with growing and running my company, I failed to do much long-term planning. Heck, the sum of my business planning extended to what new products should be offered for the next holiday.

This lack of planning also began to affect my bank accounts— both personal and the company's. I had done what most experts strongly advise against using one's own money to build a company. As soon as I received a paycheck, most of it went into the company's bank account for supplies, rent, and all too often, payroll. Turns out, using my own money left me blind to the many small cracks in my company's existence.

As the company grew, the need for capital grew, which made my day job even more important. The constant tension between my day job and the business needing capital and my time to manage and grow the business was utterly exhausting. Eventually, those small cracks would become too deep to repair.

PART 2

What I had not realized during my foray into chocolate, was that I was trapped head deep IN my business. This resulted in virtually no time to work ON my business. Even with three or four staff members who helped with production, shipping, and customers, I was doing pretty much everything else—marketing and sales, ordering, bookkeeping, banking, and deliveries. Just thinking about all the work required to keep my growing company moving forward became overwhelming. These effects can be especially acute for those solo business owners—this was huge for me. I had no one to talk to about my challenges or frustrations—it was very isolating at times.

WORKING IN YOUR BUSINESS

As a business consultant, I see this situation play out way too often, and because I lived it for nine years, I can spot it from a mile away. This business "style" leads to increased stress, frustration, debt, poor decision-making, and burnout—not to mention the strain on one's overall physical and mental health. I gained over 20 pounds, worked seven days a week, often 12–15-hour days, and survived off frozen burritos and mac-and-cheese. This way of life, my friends, is no way to run a business—nor is it sustainable.

Constantly working IN your business leaves very little time for the long-term planning that is vital for any business to be successful. I am not talking about 10 to15-year planning, which is also important, but rather more like 1 to2 year planning. Business owners I meet who are actually doing some advanced planning, typically have the bandwidth for about three to six months of planning. And yes, that is better than no planning at all.

WHY WORK ON YOUR BIZ?

Does any of this sound like you? If you have a relatively new business, constantly working IN your business may be necessary at the very beginning—I get it. But this should only be a short-term solution. You need to have a plan for how to transition yourself out of this phase.

Business owners are generally people who are very good at getting things done—we are the doers! This is a stellar trait if starting and running a business, but this trait can result in a sort of tunnel vision. We just want to complete that one task, mark it done, and go on to the next one. The process can become very addictive, but also exhausting.

Don't get me wrong, I am not saying that you should never work IN your business—that is just not realistic. However, please do have some sort of plan for working ON your business. Depending on your schedule, maybe this is blocking out an hour every morning to review your business goals, think about the next several years, or work on a specific business-related problem that needs solving. It's a time to look at things with a fresh perspective. As business owners, we tend to get so caught up in the day-to-day needs of the business, we don't prioritize time to step back and assess the direction of our business.

By consciously and consistently setting aside time regularly to focus on your business, you are providing yourself space—space to think, space to ponder and wonder, space to plan.

PART 3

You may identify with some of what I have shared about my own experiences or know someone with a similar story. Unfortunately, it took me years to realize I did not need to keep running my business by trial and error. At the time, my greatest weakness as a business owner was not knowing when to seek professional help! This was especially true for lead generation.

Unfortunately, back then, I had no clue there were business consultants who could help me with my challenges. It was only years later that I learned about many of the strategies, including lead generation strategies, that I now use to help other business owners create successful businesses.

Because I have always wanted to help people, being a business consultant is extremely rewarding. I know what it is like to constantly struggle, to feel alone in one's business, and have no one around who understands the challenges being faced on any given day. As a business consultant, I can make a difference on a much larger scale, because I am helping business owners create thriving, successful businesses. When this happens, not only are the owners happier and less stressed and have more time for family and friends, but they also have more time to work ON their business instead of constantly IN their business. When a business is financially successful, there are also greater resources to ensure employees are well-compensated, which leads to happy staff who stay around.

One of the most frequent challenges I hear from business owners is that of lead generation. Not enough qualified leads, not enough lead conversions, or difficulty maintaining a consistent flow of leads. During my chocolate days, this was one of my biggest challenges. We were constantly chasing leads in an attempt to increase revenue. It was a seemingly never-ending cycle that ultimately contributed to our demise.

This is why I have created several programs to help business owners transform the lead generation process for their business. The typical process can be expensive and extremely time-consuming. With the prevalence of various social media platforms, the business marketing landscape seems more complicated than ever. It does not need to be this way!

Business owners need a simple, no-nonsense lead generation system. A system that attracts not only leads but high-quality leads. A system with messaging that helps you engage with your ideal clients. A system with information and offers that are tailored and made for your ideal client.

If such a system might be helpful to your business, I would love for you to check out my free webinar that explains more about how business owners can easily transform their lead generation process, while making more money and working less. You can find this webinar at:

www.threesecretstogeneratingmorequalifiedprospectsfor yourbusiness.com

Over the years, I have learned a great deal, not only from my businesses and corporate background, but also from others in my field—my mentors, coaches, and teachers. As such, I believe it's my moral obligation to help business owners learn what I know and help them avoid the many mistakes I have made along the way.

Wishing you much success!

Dennis Kearney

DR. TUMBAGA

*This is Dedicated to my Beloved Mother Charlotte
who inspired me to become a physician.*

VANITY OR NOT...
DO WE REALLY NEED AESTHETIC TREATMENTS?

by Dr. Tumbaga

When I was younger, I would tell myself and my friends, "I will never get Botox!" I am guilty of judging others for receiving beauty treatments! I used to think that anyone who would get Botox and fillers was vain or narcissistic! I was so wrong! People tell me, "I want to age naturally without Botox!" The mentality and stigma I had towards Botox and other aesthetic treatments was due to how the media portrayed them. For example, let's take the Kardashians, who are known on social media to have had aesthetic injectable treatments such as lip fillers. Many people would make comments and say, "I don't want duck lips or look like a chipmunk." As an Anti-aging physician, my response would be, "of course not, who wants to look like an animal, but I don't look like an animal and I have done many aesthetic treatments on myself over the years."

Growing up I never felt beautiful, in fact, I was always shy and would hide behind my hair. This all stems from my upbringing. I lacked confidence throughout my life, even though I had overcome many obstacles to get to where I am today. Growing up in Hawaii as an orphan, I didn't have a stable family life. And so, in my journey toward becoming a physician, I discovered that I wanted to be able to help people heal themselves through self-love.

I lacked confidence in myself and never thought I would even graduate from high school since I was basically homeless at the age of 18 and uncertain of my future. Fortunately, I studied hard in high school and was able to obtain a scholarship and was able to go to college.

I thought I was on the right track, however, because I was working two jobs to support myself while attending college, it took a toll on my grades. I started my first semester with a 2.8 GPA! I found myself extremely depressed and, after that semester, I had to make some changes. I never had a low GPA like that in high school, but I later realized that I just wasn't studying as I should have been. I finally put the time into my studies and was able to get accepted into the nursing program at the University of Hawaii. It was amazing, and I loved my career as a nurse. I even started to volunteer in Humanitarian Missions all around the world and volunteered at a clinic for the indigent.

Life was great, and after a few years of Humanitarian work, I decided that I wanted to become a Humanitarian Physician. I changed my goals and started the process to take the perquisites for medical school. That too was a journey in itself! That journey led me to find out that my own philosophies and character was not what I wanted as a physician. In fact, I felt trapped.

Honestly, the training as a physician nearly killed me! I learned that Western medicine wasn't for me. And so, I had my own issues, health issues that I was dealing with, and more particularly dealing with how to care for myself. Culturally too, I would always put others first and neglect myself. And so, this is why I started my own medical clinic to be able to empower other patients by educating them on anti-aging treatments so that they also care for themselves in a manner that will lead to self-healing.

I was my first patient! I revisited the thought of getting Botox and dermal fillers. I researched those products and looked at the science behind them and why people did it. It is a medication that requires a physician's prescription and has been around since 2002 and is very safe to use when properly administered.

I took the plunge and went for it, enrolled in a training course by one of the leading physicians in aesthetics, and received treatment myself while learning more about it. After my treatment, I experienced, first-hand, what Botox, a purified protein, could do for me; dynamic wrinkles were gone! I noticed the laugh line creases softened. I felt my confidence level rising as I would now speak up more in larger groups and social events without feeling I was the ugliest person in the room.

My transformation made me realize that I was still myself after the cosmetic injections and did not look like a duck or chipmunk! This led me to believe that it was all in the technique and evaluation of the person injecting. I dispelled my prior belief that these treatments were for narcissistic and vain people, not true at all.

In my practice, I treat many prominent business owners and people in the community who have also received these treatments, and they by no means fit the Kardashian trend. They are not superficial in any way and, in fact, we share similar beliefs on how looking good physically is important. They seek our services at our clinic because of how natural they look after receiving cosmetic treatments. During the initial consultation, my team and I take a customized approach. I start by asking the patient what bothers them the most and then we educate the patient on what the treatment options are whether it's surgical or non-surgical.

We first get to know the patient and ask questions about their lifestyle and some of their common complaints such as wrinkles, laugh lines, under-eye bags, or dark spots. From there, we educate on the aging process.

For example, let's take a woman in her fifties with mature skin and volume loss to the cheeks and under her eyes. We explain that as we age the facial fat starts to diminish and the bone structures are changing, no fault of our own. It's beyond our control that the facial structures are changing; it could be partly due to hormonal changes. Unfortunately, the fat pads that atrophy or shrink in the face are one area where we don't want to lose fat, especially in the midface area (eyes, cheeks). However, we offer treatments that will allow restoration of volume loss and can rejuvenate the midface to give a more refreshed appearance.

People will not know what you had done but will comment and say, "there is something different about you." And then the patient who doesn't want to disclose what they had done, responds by saying, "Oh, thank you, I've been just getting more rest." This is what we expect will happen after we perform our aesthetic treatments...patients tell us this all the time!

During my younger years growing up in Hawaii, I took for granted that I was young and never really took good care of my skin as I do now. I rarely used or reapplied sunscreen as I was a beach island girl and loved my dark tan skin. As I got older and moved to the mainland, I didn't get as much sun exposure. However, when I would go back to Hawaii to visit, of course, I would hit the beaches and continue my same lack of skincare and application of quality sunscreen! Guess what? My skin remembered the abuse, and every time I would go back home and hit the beach, I would get patches of sunspots like a raccoon! It was so embarrassing! My eyebrow waxing person would ask me, "What happened to you?" and I would just lay there and say it's from the sun. Fortunately for me, that was a wake-up call to take better care of my skin and protect it from the sun, especially living in California. I thought to myself, how will my patients take me seriously, or would just be looking at my raccoon eyes? It took me about 2 years to get rid of the large dark spots. I had to put effort into caring for my skin and it paid off! Right now. I just have a few tiny spots, but nothing like the raccoon eyes I had.

Another reason why some people seek aesthetic treatments is to soften up an undesired look. For example, there is something called, RBF, also known as, "Resting Bitch Face." RBF! Often-times, women come in and tell us, "my husband or people always thinks I am mad," or "I have been told I always look angry," but really, they are not.

Wrinkles from scowling can contribute to these comments and affect us indirectly, and to some extent be a deterrent to our business or personal lives. Botox can help alleviate the RBF look and over time prevent static lines, also known as "elevens" from forming. We call it "11's" because they look like the number 11 in between the eyes.

The goal of these treatments is not to look 20 when you are in your 50s but to help to rejuvenate the face and age gracefully, meaning look like the younger version of yourself. In retrospect, having performed many aesthetic treatments on me along with many patients over the years, seeing the positive effect on people made me realize what a difference those treatments made. I let the patients know that I will not "overdo it" and my job is to only enhance their natural beauty. After trusting me with the treatments, I notice the patients see their natural results and you can see immediately their faces light up with confidence.

If you were like me in believing the people who had aesthetic procedures performed on them were only vain people and believed that it would not help your appearance and confidence, I would like to challenge you to change your mindset and be open to learning more about aesthetic treatments.

Botox and dermal fillers are not the only aesthetic treatments to help slow the aging process. There are many other treatments that do not include Botox and fillers such as laser, micro-needling, peel threading, medical grade skincare, plasma pen, facials,etc. We can even use your own serum and make natural fillers!

Our clinic started with me being my first patient, and once I made the transformation myself, I was able to serve my community by allowing them to make a transformation, not only physically, but increase their level of confidence as well.

No doubt that we are all aging, and can't stop the process; however, we can certainly slow it down and enhance our own beauty while looking natural without people knowing we even had an aesthetic treatment done. I guarantee that if you do as little as one thing we recommend, you will not only improve slowing the aging process, but you will certainly make a transformation that will change your thoughts on Aesthetic medicine. The mirror effect will take place, once you start to look good and feel good about your appearance, other people will want to know what you are doing and they will notice the transformation as well.

If you would like to see examples of how aesthetics treatments should look, please visit my website

www.wellnessdiagnosticsmedispa.com

or go to my Facebook business page to see the transformations we have achieved using our approach to applying aesthetic techniques. Please join my Facebook group to learn more about self-care aesthetic treatments to help you age gracefully. I look forward to seeing you there!

https://linktr.ee/extraordinaryyou

DR. POLLY HEIL-MEALEY

*To my wonderful supportive husband, Steve. I could
not be making these ripples without you!*

WHY THE STANDARD OF CARE IS NOT THE MAGIC BULLET

by Dr. Polly Heil-Mealey

Getting into the elevator on December 21, 1998, was like treading through sludge. My husband Laurence and I had just left the ENT office, where the doctor told us that Laurence had esophageal cancer. Cancer... what a horrible word. Four days before Christmas, and there was no ho, ho, ho to be found. Our two young teenage children had no knowledge that their father was ill. The timing was terrible.

What started with esophageal cancer progressed to brain cancer. He had the tumor removed from the esophagus on New Year's Eve, 1998, stayed the requisite number of days in the hospital and was released in due time. Things progressed from January until March when we took the children to the beach for spring break. Laurence was gaining weight, eating, working... things were getting back to normal.

I will never forget that spring break trip. The weather was miserable. It was cold and rainy. The sea was raging. We could not go out and were experiencing some cabin fever. Here we were on vacation at the beach in a hotel room with nothing to do. The shore was within walking distance, the fishing pier right outside our room, but the weather was just not conducive to outdoor activities. Besides the outside being gloomy, the inside was gloomy too. Laurence was not feeling well. He was dizzy and his speech was beginning to slur. I knew what to look for in terms of stroke, and he was not exhibiting any other symptoms. We decided to cut the holiday short and return home.

The first outing we took was to the emergency room. There, the doctor told us that Laurence had had a small stroke, and referred us to the local hospital. After he was admitted to the local hospital, the neurologist came and did a thorough exam. Nothing conclusive, but they did not think that he'd had a stroke. More days of testing revealed a brain tumor at the base of his skull. The neurologist referred us to a cancer specialist. This specialist told us that chemotherapy after surgery was the only option. This meant that in the slim chance that he was in the 25%, he would survive the cancer, but an infected hangnail would be too much for him to overcome.

Of course, we were referred to the best brain surgeon in the medical center for treatment of the brain cancer. The surgeon had years of vast experience and was full of hope for our future. On our part, we prayed and prepared for the big day of surgery. At the time, I was the head English teacher in a parochial school. The day before the surgery was Chapel Day, and I spent almost the entire period in the lady's restroom, on my knees, with my nose in the corner, praying for the surgeon's hands.

The next day, sitting in the waiting room while surgery was being performed, was also a day full of prayer. After the operation, the surgeon came into the waiting room and said, "The tumor just popped out of the brain like a hard-boiled egg. I wish all my patients had that type of response." We were relieved and exhausted. However, the doctor said, there were some "hot spots" in the brain that needed to be stopped with radiation so that the cancer would be halted. Operating in the dark, we followed the doctor's orders.

The radiation done as a precaution ended up taking his life. Because I was bombarded with wave after wave of extreme emotional and physical loss, I was compelled to study health and healing in a way I had previously ignored. I was plagued with questions: What did we do wrong? What could we have done, had we known more? Why was the treatment not only ineffective, but also hastened his death? The answers to these questions and more propelled me to know the truth about health and healing. I did not know the statistic that people who have cancer and do nothing medically, outlive cancer patients who opt for chemo and radiation by several years. I did not know that people with cancer were more likely to die of medical intervention rather than actual cancer.

What did we do wrong? We did not do much research on our own as we were plunged headfirst into "Standard of Care." We trusted the doctors.

1. We did not know that the medical system teaches doctors to **label diseases based on symptoms** and then prescribe drugs to mask or suppress those symptoms.

2. We did not know that chemotherapy or radiation **only worked on three cancers**: childhood leukemia, testicular cancer, and non-Hodgkin's lymphoma.

3. We did not know about the **"standard of care."** Standard of Care is what every doctor is required to do given a set of parameters of illness. There is little consideration for the actual patient's unique needs.

4. What we did not know was that any amount of radiation can cause **radiation sickness**. Though the doctors and staff were very kind, and I believe held no malice, the effects of

the radiation on the brain proved too much for Laurence's body to handle.

I wish I had known about holistic modalities when we were overwhelmed with the "C" word. All we knew was that the diet had to change.

1. We did not know that there were certain systems that held priority in the human body.

2. We did not know that if the sodium/potassium pump in each cell was not working properly that the body *could not* get well.

3. We did not know that the body was an electromagnetic organism that needed minerals and water to provide its functional ability.

Is pursuing natural, holistic health an easy path? No. The second law of thermodynamics states that all things left to themselves lead to atrophy (gradual decline in effectiveness or vigor due to underuse or neglect.) Simply put, anything left to itself will move toward disorder, disease, and chaos. Take for example an abandoned building. Left alone, within a matter of weeks or months, the building becomes overgrown with vegetation, which breaks down the structure of the building. If not tended to, within a year, the building will be falling apart, almost hidden by the growth of weeds, brambles, small trees, and the like.

So, it is with our bodies. If not tended to purposefully—with intent—then age, contamination (both environmental (chemical) and natural (parasites, germs, and bacteria), and stress will take their toll. We must, **on purpose**, treat our bodies as the organic machines that they are, tending to them, repairing them, and feeding them the correct nutrients daily so that the body will have the necessary ingredients for a long and productive life.

We all can choose how we live. We can do what is easy, eating the Standard American Diet (SAD) with all its processed nutrient sparse offerings, or we can choose healthy, holistic, organic meals full of dense nutrition. Because we do not know these things, we are not building our health.

We break our body down through many things:

1. The processed foods we eat (dead vs. live food)
2. Poor food choices we make (too many bad fats; not enough fruits and vegetables)
3. Living in a polluted atmosphere
4. Ignoring the benefit of rest
5. Unresolved negative stress

But it doesn't have to be this way! Each day we offer transformational help and education to the people we see in our clinic. You can be a ripple to change your life and the lives of people you know and love. Maybe this is the first time you have heard of holistic practices. We invite you to learn the latest in technology and education to make a real difference in your and your family's lives. We know that if the body is given the right tools in terms of nutrition, then the body can heal itself. We understand that if we can get the parents to understand how the body functions, those waves will ripple throughout the rest of the family. We are a part of transformational health every day. Feel free to look at the testimonials on our website, watch our YouTube channel, and listen to our podcasts. If you are really ready to transform your health, we invite you to take our free class:

https://whatiswrongwithmythyroid.com/

DEBORAH SMART

Dedicated to the memory of Willie Smart.

BORN TO WIN NOT RETIRE

by Deborah Smart

The biggest challenge many have is answering the question, "Should I Retire?" Having a solid retirement plan through your workplace or small business is wise. You know your future is secure.

But is it?

I worked for 17 years in corporate and have a stipend retirement income of $265 a month. My 401K went to purchasing my first home, which went through foreclosure in 2010 after my tenants could not pay rent. I was married and living with my husband, Willie. My tenant lost his job, and his wife was an entrepreneur. I allowed them to stay without paying rent until they could get back on their feet. Unfortunately, that did not happen. I could not keep up the mortgage payments and executed a short sale. I came away with an unusable settlement amount. It shocked my attorney and the realtor who handled the process. My settlement was $40,000, $30,000 the exact amount my tenants owed me, plus an additional $10,000. I tell this story because it shows why I believe the Lord orchestrates my steps through a morning routine that is devoted to Him.

I lost my husband, Donald Karper, to cancer in 2003. In 2005, I wrote a small booklet, *"Joy Comes Through the Mourning,"* because of a challenge given by my pastor. He preached on the "Parable of the Talents," gave a group of us money, and told us to do what we wanted with it. My amount was $20. I took it and purchased supplies. I printed my story, "Joy" and sold it at a fashion show. When the time came to turn the money in, I turned in $100.00 ($80 profit plus the $20 he gave me).

I expanded my story from that booklet to publishing my paperback, *"Joy Comes Through the Mourning,"* in 2011. It told the full story of my four years as a widow; how I took myself in 2004 to Bermuda for seven days, away from everyone I knew, to decide if I wanted to get married again. I realized I did not like being alone. That following year at our 2005 watch night service, I met Willie Smart. The book ends with our courtship and wedding. Willie was my joy placed in my life by the Lord.

As I was approaching 70 in 2020, I was caring for Willie. He had been in poor health since 2009. I needed to decide, "Do I retire? Do I put my full focus on caring for Willie? Do I continue working as a full-service publisher?"

I continued my morning devotion, writing in my journal for 90 days and talking to the Lord. This was my way of praying each day and focusing on my options. I turned 70 in June, and the message I received was clear. "You were born to win, not retire."

Now I don't want you to get the wrong idea. I am not saying if you retire; you are a loser. The message was specifically for me. The Lord had me on a path that I had to honor. From 2005 to 2008, I attended school and was certified as a Bible Counselor with my church. During that time until 2020, I attended our Bible Institute and earned many unaccredited credits learning the Bible. I even delivered two sermons during church services and taught spiritual gifts for a month at Bible Study. The Lord indeed had me trained and skilled to work with first-time writers struggling to write their painful testimonies or who struggled to tell their stories.

During the pandemic, I had a dream of building up a new community of writers. Not only would their books be published, but they would also identify the skills they needed to operate as a business and build their publishing and marketing platforms. My plan was to launch my program in January 2021.

Instead of the launch, life threw Willie and me a monkey wrench. We sat through a different training program. We had to decide which kind of dialysis he would be receiving. His kidneys were now in stage 4 renal failure. My priority was accompanying him to his different doctor's appointments and testing. Concentrating on my dream was out of the question. However, I did not give up on my dream. I focused on constructing a framework and platform which would house my community.

From 2020 to 2021, I signed up with multiple coaches to learn how to operate on social media at a high level. I successfully completed *Product Launch Formula* training with Jeff Walker. I joined *Doreen Rainey's Radical Success* program and excelled in learning about coaching and building a presence of influence and confidence.

In November 2020, I received an invitation to join Terri Levine, CEO of the *Modern Coaching Method*. She reached out to me because she recognized my potential based on my social media postings and my background. Financially, I could not take part in the program she was offering. However, I joined her heart-centered Facebook group, "Heartrepreneurs," and actively became part of the community.

In March 2021, I decided to take the month of April off as a sabbatical. I needed to examine what I should do with the rest of my career. I needed to figure out how to increase my income to help cover the potential expenses which would result from Willie's health crisis.

On the first day, I wrote my vision for the upcoming year. I ended my entry by asking the Lord, "What is it you want me to accomplish during this time?" I immediately and clearly heard, "Learn to be still." On the second day, the message was, "Learn to focus on now." And the third day, "Learn to follow the desires of YOUR heart." On the fourth day, Willie's blood sugar shot up over 500 and continued to rise. We couldn't get it down. A week later, he was hospitalized. A week after that, my older brother Avon died.

During that time, I was still focused on what I could and could not do. I also didn't allow outside pressures to overrun me. I learned only to do what was in my heart: take care of Willie. I also took care of my need to continue moving my vision quest forward. I signed up for a 30-day challenge to launch a podcast.

July 7, 2021, I launched "Smart Talks with One Smart Lady," a 30-minute podcast based on the three-tier proprietary program I designed to launch that January. My first guest was Marketing and Coaching CEO Terri Levine. Terri calls her clients "client family members." As of that July, I still had not signed up for any of Terri's programs. I told her she should consider me a "kissing cousin." She was generous with her time and consented to be on my podcast.

In addition, the timing was right. My marketing hub was complete. A marketing hub is not a website or marketing funnel. It is like Grand Central Station in New York City. It brings many people into the transportation center and directs them to the train tracks, taking them to their destination. That is how I designed "One Smart Lady Productions," my home on the internet.

Many authors and entrepreneurs have websites. A marketing hub allows you to house a website, landing pages for your multiple marketing endeavors, and your blog. No need for a standalone blog site. We are also building the ability to track your membership community. Again, no need for a stand-alone membership program. It will be integrated.

I link my guest's podcast to a resource page on the marketing hub. It expounds on who they are and how listeners can reach and stay in touch with their programs.

I had a very active year with guests graciously sharing their stories about how they "Dared to Dream," "Dare to Grow" and "Dare to Prosper" in their field of expertise.

In November, my younger brother Eric passed away. November, we began dialysis training. We selected Peritoneal Dialysis, and in December, I gave Willie his treatment at home, four times a day every day until January when he went on the machine, which cycled five times overnight every day.

On March 11, 2022, Willie passed away from End-Stage Renal Failure and other natural causes.

You would think my world ended. It didn't because if you recall, a year before, the Lord had given me my directive. Over that year, and with the level of caregiving I gave, I learned to create a sanctuary that helped me through the tragedies I experienced in 2021 and 2022.

This is the path the Lord set me on. I want to help anyone who struggles with the decision between following their vision quest and caring for a loved one. You can dare to dream, grow, and prosper as you live your life and follow your heart's desire. Connect with me. Find out more about how I help you win during your pre- and retirement years; visit https://borntowinnotretire.com.

EVA ALBERTS

I dedicate this chapter to my sons, love you all, you are my treasure, my heart is full of gratitude.

I ALMOST DIED

by Eva Alberts

Today I am creating a ripple to help women all around the world.

I am a midwife and a mother of Five. I have helped thousands of women through pregnancy and childbirth, and for the past decade, I have done more than 8000 in-home visits helping first-time mothers overcome their fear and anxiety during the first days after delivery. After my near-death experience, I became a midwife, and today I am creating a ripple as *Your Online Midwife*.

On a cold and snowy winter day in February 1977, my life was forever changed. I was 17, in college, and I had just found out that I was pregnant! Of course, it wasn't planned, I felt paralyzed when I got the result. How could I be a mother at only 17? How would I get through this? Could I finish school? Would the baby be okay? What happens next? What would my life become? I didn't know what to expect, there was no internet, social media did not exist—no easy access to information. Only books. Imagine the emotional state of a 17-year-old teenager who had not planned to become pregnant in college. I was happy, excited, scared, anxious, and stressed at the same time.

I was working at a diner in the countryside during the summer, away from my family. I felt terrible both mentally and physically. When I came back home, I developed severe pre-eclampsia. I was hospitalized with total bed rest for three terrible weeks before my son was born. I often felt like no one listened to me at the hospital. I wasn't told what was happening other than that my baby wasn't growing and I had pre-eclampsia.

I needed education and support to get through this, someone to help me emotionally. Very few health care professionals took the time to talk to me, explain things, and ask how I was feeling, but I was grateful on the few occasions someone did.

My condition got worse, and finally; the doctor decided to induce labor. It didn't work, my son's heartbeat slowed down, he was dying, and I was in a critical condition with a high risk of eclampsia. I had an emergency C-section.

The doctor cut my son's shoulder during the C-section. His weight was 1,320 gr/2.14 pounds. There were severe complications, and I was in critical condition for many days. I didn't know if my son would survive and I didn't see him until a week after delivery.

We were lucky, we both made it, but the following weeks and months were not easy. My son spent the first two months of his life at the hospital and, back in 1977, the health care system didn't provide the help and support I needed. Imagine my emotional state, the fear, and anxiety. Thank God for my mom and dad and their support.

I graduated with my classmates and went from being a helpless young mother to becoming a midwife in 1982, determined to help others who were in the same situation, and today I am still doing this for as many women as I possibly can.

How does this work?

In Iceland, all women get in-home visits from a midwife within the first 10 days if they are discharged from the hospital within the first three days after delivery. During these daily visits, they get help with breastfeeding and whatever the midwife can assist with. The midwife's role is to support, educate, answer questions, and make sure that the mother, spouse, and newborn are doing well, both mentally and physically.

What I've noticed is that parents spend a lot of time preparing for labor and birth, but when it comes to the recovery period, they're completely unprepared. Labor and birth normally take a day or two, but the postpartum recovery period takes at least six weeks.

I often get this question: "Why did no one tell me how difficult the first days after delivery are?"

The first days are challenging for both parents, both mentally and physically. It has nothing to do with how happy they are. Sleepless nights, cluster feeding, sore nipples, stitches that hurt, contractions, stress, and Baby Blues.

When the baby is born, parents are flooded with feelings, full of joy and happiness. During the first few days, fear and anxiety show up, and suddenly everything they thought they knew is tossed aside when they find themselves without answers. Why is the baby crying so much? He hasn't pooped for two days, is that normal? Am I starving my baby? Will the head always look like this? Why doesn't she want to sleep in her bed?

All of this can be overwhelming, but we tend to overcomplicate things. Often the answers are more simple than expected. My best advice is to use common sense, trust your intuition, and educate yourself as best you can. We must keep in mind that pregnancy, labor, and birth are natural processes, and so is the postpartum period. Let's look at breastfeeding as an example.

Cluster feeding is important for the mother as well as the baby during the first days. It's the perfect design by nature because the baby needs time to learn to suck the nipple instead of a finger, and breastfeeding causes the brain to release Prolactin, the milk-producing hormone, and Oxytocin, a hormone that contracts the uterus.

During these first days, the baby is losing weight and is hungry. Crying is how the newborn communicates. It's important to breastfeed every two to three hours during the first days because the baby only gets half to one teaspoon each time. The first milk, the colostrum, is very nourishing and full of antibodies. It's also recommended to check the baby's weight, because newborns lose weight in the first days, and to check if the baby has jaundice because jaundice can cause brain damage if not treated.

Breastfeeding should not be painful. The right latch is the key, both the mother and the baby need time to learn, and it requires patience and persistence. The breasts are not supposed to be full of milk on day two. The milk usually comes in on days 3,4,5 or 6, every mother and baby are different. During this process using a pacifier is not recommended because the baby is losing weight and needs the colostrum, and to stimulate milk production and contract the uterus.

Parenting is a new role, and my best advice is to be well prepared for the postpartum period. Knowing what to expect and what to do when the baby is born increases self-confidence and helps reduce fear, stress, and anxiety. Even simple things like holding the baby can be stressful.

If you, or someone you know, are expecting or just had a baby, here are a few tips:

- Plan ahead and ask for help.

- Take one day at a time, be in the moment.

- Sleep when the baby is sleeping during the day the first week or two.

- Give yourself permission to feel the way you feel.

- Make sure your emotional operating system is turned on.

- Take a few deep breaths when you are overwhelmed.

- Tell your partner how you feel and what you need.

- Ask a family member to be available to help out the first week.

- Eating, drinking, sleeping, and breastfeeding are the only things the mother should be doing during the first week or two.

The fact is, that when you get support, guidance, and education, everything works better.

In-home visits from midwives are not offered in all countries but you can just imagine how helpful these visits during the first days are, when you are on your own, insecure, starting to breastfeed, and getting to know your baby.

That's why I created the online course "*First 10 Days*", my little ripple, my little wave that I'm making to help humanity, to empower, support, and educate mothers and their families in the first days and weeks after delivery.

So, they know what to expect and why, what is normal and what isn't, what to do, and when to call a doctor. The online course provides easy access to all the information you need about the mother's physical and mental health and recovery, breastfeeding, the newborn, and more, including information for the father, siblings, family, and friends and daily support during the first days. Meditations, checklists, affirmations, answers to FAQs, and more. I recommend watching it before the baby is born. The more you know, the easier and less stressful the postpartum period will be.

My goal is to increase self-confidence, lower stress, fear, and anxiety, encourage breastfeeding, and lower the risk of post-partum depression.

As a midwife and life transformation strategist, I am passionate to educate, support, and help as many as I possibly can and preventing that first-time mother's experience that I went through in my first pregnancy. Knowledge is key.

My dream is to help one million women and their families around the world. If you like what you've read, if you or anyone you know is pregnant, here's my gift to you. Just go to my website to download it: **youronlinemidwife.com/makingwaves**

For more information and if you want to work with me: **youronlinemidwife.com**

WEBSITE: youronlinemidwife.com
EMAIL: eva@youronlinemidwife.com

Eva Alberts

KEN ATTARD

Dedicated to my beautiful daughter Ema,
may she always remember how her smile and laughter can
light up a room and the lives of those it touches.

THE INSIDE LANE

WHERE THE "UMAMI-SELF™" RESIDES

by Ken Attard

He shoots, he scores," the voice of Foster Hewitt excitedly blurts over the radio or the TV. I must have heard that expression at least a million times as a child, and I can still hear his voice in my head today.

Not surprisingly, being born in Toronto, Canada, I had skates on my tiny feet at the tender age of five, as so many Canadians do.

I thought this is my dream, hockey stardom awaits me, and I could say that up until the age of 12 that this was my track.

Evening and 6 a.m. practices, weekdays and evening games, and of course, out-of-town tournaments; it was all happening ... until it was not!

It happened suddenly, just like a cold winter blizzard would hit the streets of Toronto. I remember one specific out-of-town tournament in Ottawa when I was suddenly left on the bench by the coach. I did not know why and swirling in my head were questions like "Did I do something wrong?" or I thought "Obviously, I am not good enough anymore."

The next thing I knew, I was in my hotel bed, with both of my parents trying to console me while they were also in dismay. I was sobbing and distraught. I was 12, and for me, this was significant because things were about to change; it was a pivotal episode in my life.

Fast forward two years later, and my parents made the decision to head back to their native land of Malta after 16 years in Canada.

Okay, so now not only has the hockey dream died, but I am moving to an island that is in the middle of the Mediterranean Sea where there are not a lot of ice rinks around, actually none at all, at least not back then. This was 1979. It would be another 20 years before I would put ice skates on again.

Fast forward 47 years, where I can now write about this noteworthy experience and pivot in my life along with so many others, with not just an understanding, but rather a "knowing" that my experience back then, together with every other experience, whether it was "good" or "bad" in appearance has led me to where I am today. Together, they were the catalyst to recognizing the "essence" of who I truly am, my "Umami-Self.™"

I remember attending a retreat several years back where I was asked over and over, (as one of the exercises) "Who are you?" after answering what seemed to be a gazillion times, I finally succumbed and said, "I am Ironman" and held out the palm of my hand just like Ironman. Naturally, this brought on laughter from the individual asking me that question.

Now, it's your turn. Who are you?

Just like the 12-year-old who identified with being a hockey player and that being the equivalent of success, of being good enough, and then suddenly being distraught once that was "taken away", whom do you identify as being? Father, mother, son, husband, wife, partner, daughter, clerk, businessperson, company director, owner, athlete, friend, employee, employer ... the list goes on and on.

You may potentially identify with some of these or other "identities", and you would sincerely identify with that person or occupation.

I find it funny how you come into this world really with no identity and quite free from any attachments.

Imagine you were taking part in a race on an athletic track, and let's call that race "Life." (it's not really a race) If you had a choice of which lane you would want to be on, which one would it be, the outside lane or the inside lane? Logically, it makes sense that you would want to be on the inside lane, as this would be the shortest distance to the finish line. Comparable to when you are born without any attachments, you are still connected to where you came from, your Umami-Self.™- At this stage, you are still on the inside lane.

The word "connected" is key here. Connected, as I said, to where you came from, and something bigger than you. Some of the names this has been given include God, Source, Source Energy, The Field, The Quantum Field, and Universe to name just a few. These are all simply names, you can call it whatever you like. You can call it Bob, Bill, or Jane, it really does not matter since it is all the same. I have chosen to call it the Umami-Self™.

I coined this term when I understood the meaning of Umami in the food world, which essentially is an indescribable taste when you eat something that is so delicious. In fact, the definition of Umami is "The essence of deliciousness" and hence, the Umami-Self™ is "The Essence of Deliciousness of Who You Truly Are." When you learn to tap into that essence, it is indescribable in words. It's a place where "All Is."

So, you enter this game of life already there, where you are already on the inside lane, you are connected and then it starts! What naturally resides in you and never leaves you begins to be pushed to the side, and you begin to move towards the outside lane. You begin to be taught that you are meant to achieve accolades and that these achievements will determine your success.

Amazingly you are being taught by others, taking on their beliefs and potentially carrying them forward with you for the rest of your life. I say potentially because you have the opportunity, the choice, and the power to change that. It starts with awareness.

What is mindset? The official definition is "the established set of attitudes held by someone." What is it that you keep top of mind most of the time? Are you aware that you could have control over this? Are you aware that what you're thinking is linked to what you believe? Are you aware that the results and experiences you are creating are essentially a byproduct of your thoughts?

Information today is readily available. In one day, you can have more information at your fingertips than my grandparents could have had in a lifetime. More than likely, the fact that you are reading this means that you have heard of Mindset in one form or another, yet potentially you could still be suffering from what I call "*The Triple U Syndrome*.™"

Yes, you have heard of mindset, and you may have been very intrigued by it and got quite excited about it, yet did you give it the credit it is due? This leads you right into the first "U" which is UNDERRATED. You still underrate your mindset. Do you truly believe it is your superpower to create the results and experiences you want for your career, relationships, wealth, growth, and your best life, or would you leave it on the back burner or on the shelf like a purchased book that you have never read? Just like the book, you literally only need to pull it off the shelf and start reading. You simply need to start to be consistent with your awareness regarding mindset.

This leads us right into the second "U" which is "UNDERESTI-MATED." Since you underrate your mindset, you automatically underestimate it, again, not giving it the time of day that it deserves.

Okay, okay, so let me let you off the hook. It's not your fault! You underrate and underestimate the power of your mindset because up until now you do not have a strong enough belief in it. This lack of belief ultimately then creates the third "U" which is "UNDERUTILIZE." You refrain from tapping into your superpower.

I mean, think about it, you most likely have been taught all your life that if you want to be successful, you need to be prepared to struggle, sacrifice, suffer, and be stressed! Life is difficult. Does that sound familiar? You have been consistently pushed to the outside lane where everything that counts is outside of you.

Let's say you are the individual that is on the outside lane. I call that person the "Acquisition Accomplisher." You are going to sprint as hard and fast as you can to acquire as much as possible because that is where your identity comes from. Now, let me make something very clear, there is nothing "wrong" in accomplishing and acquiring. The challenge is when you get so attached to those acquisitions and solely identify with them. If that is the case, then you will be continuously chasing for more, and there will never be enough to satisfy that identity, and this then leads to struggle, sacrifice, suffering, and stress. You will do anything to lift that trophy and say, "I made it" and then not long after, you will find yourself saying "Now what?"

Now, let's say you are the individual on the inside lane. I call that person the "Unattached Accomplisher." Your journey is not a constant sprint to accomplish. Sometimes you do sprint, yet sometimes it's a jog, interval training, or maybe a walk. More often than not, it's like riding one of those Trav-O-Lator machines (flat escalators) like they have in airports, just floating along, taking you to your next destination in a comfortable and easy manner. Your life is now filled with more fun, inspiration, fulfillment, and impact rather than mostly suffering, sacrifice, struggle, and stress. You have tapped into the Umami-Self™.

I ask you again, "Who are you?" and more importantly, "Who do you want to become?"

As an outside lane master, you are closer to the bleachers where the crowds are more predominant. You depend on the input from the crowds for your success or downfall. A continuous seeking of external validation, your power lies outside of you because it comes mainly from the crowd.

As an inside lane master, you are closer to the very inner part of the track where your coaches, mentors, and other athletes are stationed. They guide and keep you focused on the inside lane, keep you true to yourself, and keep you connected to your Umami-Self™ where everything you want resides. Your power lies within you and depends solely on you and nobody else, where you know you are worthy regardless of what anyone else says.

I believe it is imperative to note that whatever lane you choose, you will always get to the finish line. Every lane leads to the same place, the difference being that the closer you are to the inside lane, the easier and more joyful you make the journey for yourself. I like to make things as easy and as simple as possible by helping others realize they can do it for themselves.

You might be saying this sounds great yet, "Ken, how do I begin to tap into my Umami-Self?"™

3 SIMPLE TIPS

1. APPRECIATE EVERY DAY. List 3-5 (things/people/anything) that you appreciate. Start an Appreciation Journal and ideally, make this list first thing in the morning.

2. TAKE THE TIME TO LEARN ABOUT MINDSET EVERY DAY. Be consistent. Let me start you off. Go to successfulentrepreneurnow.com. Entrepreneur or not, you will benefit from this.

3. STOP. Take quiet time and time to be on your own EVERY day. If you do the math, one hour a day for 365 days is equivalent to 42 eight-hour days. This is where inspiration happens!

I would like to let you move on from here with this understanding. No one person is more significant than another. You and I and everyone is the same at our essence, the Umami-Self™. You may not feel it yet, still, I can guarantee that the ember within can never go out. It only takes that one tiny ember to rekindle the light within.

You are beautiful as you are,

there is nothing to fix,

and you are exactly where you are meant to be right now.

All is perfect.

You are loved.

LYSSA JAYE

For my amazing parents, who've always believed in me and who showed me that it is never too late to follow my dreams or impact people's lives. I love you.

A SINGLE DROP: THE RIPPLE EFFECT FROM HEALTHCARE TO WELLCARE

by Lyssa Jaye

The fire starts in my chest and flows outward; blood boils to the surface of my skin and sweat trickles down my spine. My heart racing, my face burning, I take a deep centering breath, grateful for the cool metal of the exam-room doorknob. It's time to ignore my perimenopausal inferno and give my attention and care to Gina, a 48-year-old woman sitting on an exam table, naked from the waist down, covered only by a tissue-thin sheet of paper. Gina. My 19th patient of the day.

Aware of clinic time constraints, Gina quickly lists her concerns: Unexplained weight gain, trouble sleeping, constant fatigue, nightly doom-scrolling, no libido (and a resentful partner), gushing periods every 3-4 weeks, vaginal irritation, gassy bloating, and a funky smell "down there." Sometimes she gets hot for no reason and finds it hard to focus. She has a special-needs tween who's in multiple types of therapy, and two older kids for whom she is mostly a chauffeur. She's covering two jobs for the same pay because a co-worker quit. She's had repeat vaginal infections over the past few years, and each time she's been given a one-week course of oral antibiotics. Her family lives on takeout pizza, Chinese food, and burritos. Gina is funny, making me laugh more than once; she takes pride in her career and is dedicated to her family. She is also so, so very tired.

She tells me all of this while I am busily doing her pap smear and breast exam. She's unfazed by my multitasking. She's had endless similar conversations at similar appointments in similar clinics; she has no expectation that today will be any different, or that her concerns will ever be adequately addressed.

Nevertheless, I persist. At lightning speed, I share some tips to get better sleep and recommend some very basic lab work that will give us hints (but not clear answers) and may lead to a referral to a primary care provider, which she does not have. I empathize and briefly explain the process of perimenopause and why we want to check her thyroid. I treat her recurrent infection with local antibiotic gel, tout the benefits of probiotics, and suggest ways to prevent reinfection. I print out a mammogram referral and information sheets for her to read at home. When I suggest she could meditate daily, Gina throws me a sardonic side-eye. I encourage her to come back for another visit, for which she'll have to take another afternoon off from work, to review lab results and discuss specific lifestyle changes and possible hormone treatment from a limited formulary approved by her insurance.

Our 10 minutes are up. Bidding her a rushed farewell, I have five minutes to chart a complete note, splash cool water on my face, and take another centering breath so I can give all my attention and care to my 20th patient of the day. There are 6 more left to see. I pass them in the waiting room, checking their watches, fidgeting, staring at their phones, and shushing irritable kids because they don't have childcare. It is 4:30 pm. It will be another late evening and several more anxiety-induced hot flashes for me. Worse, most of these women will leave with a quick fix for an acute issue but without the comprehensive, in-depth care they desperately need.

It took years of working in hospitals and family-planning clinics, my own raging perimenopause symptoms that my doctor ignored, and a worldwide pandemic for me to figure out that I could not continue. It wasn't just burnout. It was a profound realization that in our sick-care system, I was never going to fulfill my calling to help women achieve true, lasting, vibrant health. Worse, the act of trying was destroying my own well-being.

Wellness isn't just the absence of illness or the temporary easing of symptoms. It is feeling strong, sleeping well, and nourishing bodies with good foods and thoughts; it is balance and happiness, peace of mind, and the ability and desire to engage with work, friends, and family. It is living in a body that feels right and can do what is needed and desired. It is knowing that from the inside out, our cells, organs, hormones, and systems are functioning optimally. It is aging well, building resiliency, maintaining energy, and knowing how to prevent or mitigate future health problems. When women have this type of health, their families, communities, and workplaces thrive.

We, women, are the linchpins of our families. When I lived in India, I saw how donations from organizations were directed to women, because we can be depended on to pay it all forward. Wherever we are, if we have resources, we use them to improve the lives of not just our families, but our villages, and, ultimately, our entire societies. The same goes for health: Well women use their energy, vigor, and drive to enrich the lives of those around them.

Women's health also ripples out into their wider communities, as we become leaders who uplift others at work, undertake creative endeavors, or volunteer and lead in schools, spiritual spaces, and community programs. As women flourish, so do their worlds.

I see this time and again: Women who project confidence, who are the rock everyone depends on, who balance it all—and behind the curtain, they're pushing past disruptive symptoms, exhaustion, joint pain, brain fog, fatigue, digestive problems, hormone fluctuations, anxiety or depression, and a million other health issues to meet the bare minimum of their obligations. Days are a straight line from caffeine, to sugar, to wine, to sleeping pills. They do it all but feel like they do none of it well because there's never time, energy, or money to fill their own buckets. I knew I could do more to help these women.

I tried to pack education, motivation, and advice that would address the fullness of each woman's needs into every interaction at the clinic. But as the man said in the Broadway show Hamilton, "If there's a fire you're trying to douse, you can't put it out from inside the house." I needed to step outside and find a different, better way to a reimagined health care paradigm. I upended the type of care I provide—from chaotic clinic visits to the serenity of functional medicine—and it transformed my life and the health of the women I see; I believe I'll be part of a tide that transforms the entire landscape of healthcare in this country.

In my private practice, **Positively Thriving, Functional Wellness for Women,** I spend time with each client, getting to know her and her history, and giving her the in-depth care she deserves. I empower each to overcome her unique health issues, and I guide her on a personalized path to optimal health and a better quality of life. I don't treat a pile of symptoms. I connect the dots to reveal the root causes of imbalances in the body through a unique and comprehensive medical history and targeted lab tests. I then address these underlying causes with changes to mindset, diet, sleep, exercise, and supplementation —and yes, we still utilize prescription medications and specialists when needed.

The women I now see in my practice come to me when it has all become too much. From their sporadic and disconnected doctor appointments, they have nothing to show but some prescription bottles, snide advice to lose weight, and a general sense of resignation that it's all downhill from wherever they are. It's not enough. They want more. And that's what I provide.

What if Gina came to Positively Thriving? Let's imagine it: I'm waiting calmly for her at my uncluttered desk in a sunny, tranquil room. Gina strolls in exactly when her appointment is promised, and we sip tea in comfy chairs. I've read her intake forms and I'm ready to get to know her. She runs down every momentous occurrence in her life—every antibiotic, infection, trauma; every joy, triumph, a moment of clarity—while I map it on a timeline. We delve into her diet, habits, lifestyle, sleep patterns, how and when she moves her body, what causes her stress, and how she responds. We chart when each symptom started and what may have triggered it. I listen closely to her fears, her concerns, what brings her joy, and what makes her sad—I may even sit and hold space as she cries. Finally, we discuss her health goals and how I will help her reach them.

This two-hour visit is the first intake and, as we work together over the following months, Gina feels heard and seen, confidently makes health-boosting changes, and feels stronger, more energetic, happier, and healthier. Her family is thriving; her kids are responding to the healthy food and Gina's reduced stress; they meditate with her and have become more appreciative of their time together. Her relationship with her partner is more loving, less reactive, and includes more intimacy. She has been promoted at work and has started mentoring the younger generation. She volunteers at the school and has joined a book club, expanding her social circle—with new friends excited to follow in her new-healthy footsteps. Her life has been transformed. And because I'm delivering this type of care to women, so has mine.

CONNECT WITH ME

Facebook:

https://www.facebook.com/groups/navigatingthechange

Consumer Awareness Guide:

http://www.howtobalanceyourhormones.com

Take The Course:

http://www.naturalhormonebalance.com

If you are interested in this type of healthcare, please book a free 15 minute consultation call at:

https://positivelythriving.md-hq.com/embedded/schedule. php.

Lyssa Jaye

MARTHA DAVIS ALEXANDER

To my husband Greg for all his love and support; and a big Thank you to Terri Levine for the invitation to be part of this book.

THE RIPPLES OF CHANGE: THE PEOPLE PLEASER'S FORMULA FOR AN ABUNDANT LIFE

by Martha Davis Alexander

I am a recovering people pleaser. I became a people pleaser the day I came home and my dad told me my mom had left and taken two of my three older brothers with her. I was seven years old. It became my job, purpose, and focus to make sure I was lovable and likable so that I would never be abandoned again. My life was filtered through my desperation to be accepted and loved. I did not believe I was worthy of love. After all, my own mom left me. I learned to change my personality like a chameleon changes his skin to adapt to my surroundings and the people I was around. As a result, I developed superpowers: I can read a room of people and instantly know where the emotional landmines are; I can easily adapt to fit almost any situation and I can read between the lines. I often see truths others miss.

The mindset I created on that beautiful summer day in 1968 remained fully intact and my primary focus for more than 50 years. It was the invisible filter by which I viewed the world and those around me. It was how I made most of my decisions, without even realizing it. The mindset was clear, I had to do something or be someone different. During all that time, I did not know who I was or what I wanted. I did not live my life intentionally. I went whichever way I thought I could find security, safety, and acceptance. I did not value my time or my efforts, so I volunteered for EVERYTHING and undervalued my business services. I believed that if I did enough, gave enough, and offered services for way less than the market value, I would be ok. The search for safety, security, love, and acceptance was the sole focus of my being. My singular focus left no time or energy for dreams, visions, or my life purpose. I did not have an abundant life.

What was the cost of my people pleasing? The cost to me was immense. I did not know who I was or what I wanted. I felt overwhelmed, exhausted, frustrated, resentful, and anxious. I was constantly monitoring my behavior and actions. The struggle became so much that I started to think daily about suicide as the way out of my misery. I knew there was so much more to life. My life purpose felt like it was slipping through my grasp. I worked hard at my business and never made headway. I thought I was showing up, networking, and putting myself out there. My services were priced under the market. And yet, I did not build a profitable business.

The cost to my family was that I was not truly available to them. I was always busy trying to be someone else in an effort to be liked. I was not present with them, and my depression was a wall around me. I fell short as a role model for my children. They learned to be anxious and to people please. I didn't teach them that they are powerful, resourceful, and perfectly imperfect. We could not discuss difficult issues without anger and resentment.

In 2019 my self-control diminished to almost nothing. I was left embarrassed and frequently cleaned up after my outbursts of bent-up rage, resentment, anger, and fear. In August of 2019, I saw a Facebook post of a dear friend whom I knew had struggled as well. She had found her answer, and I wanted that answer too. I immediately enrolled in a life coach certification course that started to change my life. The ripples of change that spread as I stepped into the freedom to love and accept my authentic self were magical. Now, I am happy and filled with joy. I no longer worry if someone is going to like or love me. They do or they don't; either is fine with me because I love and like myself. My family is much happier. We have clear and effective communication and rarely have anger and resentment when having discussions, even about money. My kids have seen me work to personally develop a healthier, happier life. I am a true friend. I no longer carry resentment and anger, I give out of love, and the desire to serve others, rather than out of a need for security, love, or being liked and accepted. I have a life of abundance.

My business now has a solid foundation based upon who I am as my authentic self. I have clients who value my services and are willing and able to pay. I do not hesitate to state my fees. I do not offer discounts for my services. I know who I am, the services I offer, and the value of my services. I show up networking as my authentic self and have so much more fun than ever before. I make true long-term connections that are mutually beneficial because of genuine care.

 If you identify with my story, it is likely that you are a people pleaser. The first step towards your abundant life is for you to decide if you are a people pleaser. Here is a simple test for to you can take. Answer the following questions, yes or no (note: if the statement resonates with you the answer is yes).

Do you:

1. Apologize often? Even when it is not your fault?

2. Say yes before thinking about whether you want to do something?

3. Say yes when you want to say no?

4. Feel guilty when you say no?

5. Say you agree with others even when you don't agree?

6. Avoid conflict?

7. Avoid difficult subjects?

8. Put other people's needs ahead of your needs?

9. Avoid boundaries?

10. Relive conversations repeatedly to see if you made a mistake?

11. Avoid setting intentions?

12. Struggle to know what you want?

13. Let other people tell you what you "should" want, do, say, think?

14. Struggle to dream for yourself?

15. Worry about what other people think?

What are your intentions when you do any of the above-listed actions? Is it out of genuine desire to do something without anything in return? Or is it with the intention of being accepted, liked, appreciated, and/or acknowledged? If it is the latter, and you identified strongly with more than 5 of the above statements, you are more than likely a people pleaser.

The next step is to decide if being a people pleaser is impacting your life and your business. Reflect on these questions and the resulting impact on your life and business.

- Do you long for something more and feel stuck and overwhelmed?

- Do you carry resentment, anger, and frustration when you put someone else first?

- Do you hesitate to charge what you are worth (or ask for a pay raise)?

- Do you hesitate to state your fees or the price you want?

- Do you discount your services or products to make a sale?

- When someone asks for your vision, mission statement, or dreams do you feel like a deer in the headlights?

- Do you feel like you are missing your purpose in life?

- Do you take it personally when someone says no to you, your services, or your products?

Congratulations! You are almost there. If you have decided that being a people pleaser is impacting your life/business, the fabulous news is that YOU get to choose if you want to continue to be a people pleaser or if you want to empower yourself. Being a people pleaser is not a life sentence; it is programming that can be changed. Here is my formula for empowering yourself to profitability:

THE ABUNDANCE EQUATION FOR PEOPLE PLEASERS

(authentic self + how you want to show up + values + boundaries + what you want + what brings you joy) **MINUS**

(people who are not supporting you + limiting beliefs + habits that no longer serve you) **PLUS**

(a healthy relationship with money + being gentle with yourself) = **An Abundant Life**

I spent more than 50 years as a people pleaser. Working through this formula was not done overnight. It has taken me years to work through the formula to create my abundant life. Give yourself the time, space, care, and love you would give your best friend. This journey from people pleaser to your abundant life is worth taking and each step is worth celebrating.

I support women who struggle with people pleasing and reach beyond their programming to find their abundant life. Being a people pleaser does not leave room for an abundant life. If your focus is on being loved, liked, and accepted, you are missing the bigger picture. I am here to support you on your journey of freedom from people pleaser to your life of abundance. This journey can be overwhelming, I did not make these changes alone. I had coaches, mentors, and a close circle of people going through the same process together. I am here to help you complete your journey to abundance from start to finish.

In the meantime, I have created tools so you can get started on your journey now.

1. Join the Facebook group: Becoming Courageously You at www.facebook.com/groups/849570223065931/

2. Take the free assessment at www.CourageouslyMeQuiz.com to see if you qualify for a free breakthrough session with Courageously You Coaching.

Martha Davis Alexander

| 119

REGINA ANDLER

I dedicate this chapter to mom and dad. Thank you for teaching me that I can do anything I set my mind and heart on.

UNDERSTANDING THE POWER OF YOUR ENERGY IS THE KEY TO YOUR SUCCESS

by Regina Andler

Did you ever walk into a room full of people and get an instant feeling that you didn't want to be there?

Or maybe you were out meeting with a new potential colleague and within five minutes of the conversation, you completely tuned them out?

Have you ever met someone for the first time and just knew to the depths of your being that you were meant to work with this person?

It's the energy.

Everything is energy and for me, the most fascinating energy is the energy that is sent out in ripples from every one of us every single minute of every day.

As a business owner of over 20 years, I have connected with literally thousands of people around the world and attended hundreds of networking meetings with all different types of people.

When I started my first business, I decided to attend some local networking events to drum up some business. I had no clue how to network, I just thought you get some business cards printed, sign up for an event, go to the meeting and the magic happens.

Boy, did I get that one wrong!

I knew nothing about energy back then. All I knew was that I wanted more clients for my business, and I was told I needed to go out and network to get them.

There I was, walking into my first networking event, bright-eyed and bushy-tailed and ready to conquer the world.

I will never forget that first meeting.

When I left, I felt like a steamroller had run me down like one of those cartoon characters all flattened out on the road with my edges rolling up as the steamroller passed by.

The experience was so intense that I thought I would never attend another networking meeting in my life.

Afterward, I met with a friend, who was a self-proclaimed "master networker" to see if he could give me some networking tips. He laughed when I told him my story and asked what meeting I went to.

When I told him, he rolled his eyes as he knew that particular group and said, "Yeh, they can be a nasty bunch."

I was a bit taken aback by this and asked what he meant. He knew I was looking for connections and clients for my business and he noted that this particular group was a bunch of "energy vampires"—a term I had never heard of till then.

He said all they do is push what they are selling, never ask about you and your business and most of them are fly-by business card passers—meaning they walk past you, say a quick "Hi", hand you their card without asking anything about you, grab your card and then move on to their next victim. He said, "They suck the life and energy out of everyone they come into contact with!"

That was exactly what I had experienced! And I had given a bunch of cards out that night, which turned into hundreds of spam emails that I never asked for or wanted.

None of them became clients or connections for my business.

In those early days, I learned a very valuable lesson about how energy works and I also learned that it can be one of the most valuable tools in your business toolbox, and in life.

Many years later, and much wiser, I now consider myself to be a self-proclaimed master networker.

What I did was learn how to master what I call the "inner GPS".

The inner GPS is the energy inside you that is always letting you know if something is good or not-so-good. You feel it in your emotions. You feel it when you get that hair-standing-up-on-my-neck feeling. You feel it when you "get butterflies" in your stomach. It's all energy.

I learned to pay attention to this energy and instead of just letting it flow uncontrolled, I learned how to use it and shape it to my advantage.

I learned how to shift my energy to match those that I meet to create deeper, long-lasting connections.

More recently, I attended a networking meeting and when I walked into the room, I was instantly bombarded by three women who rushed up to meet me before I could even make it to the registration table.

I checked my energy, smiled, introduced myself, and let them talk about themselves (because that is what they really wanted to do), then accepted the cards they handed (more accurately: shoved) to me, and only when they asked, did I reach into my purse for my card to give to them.

When their initial burst of energy was over, I excused myself and went to check-in.

The person running the event had seen the exchange. He apologetically smiled, and said, "They are three of our oldest members and they are always anxious to greet new people. I hope they didn't scare you away!"

I smiled and said "Of course not. It is nice that you have such an enthusiastic greeting committee."

20 years ago, I would have likely fled the event as fast as I could with my tail between my legs.

Now, I know how to recognize the energy and adjust accordingly so that it does not affect me in a negative way.

If meeting new people for your business is important to you, here are a few tips on how to make your next networking event more fun and productive for you.

First, attend with purpose. When you sign up for a networking event, set your intentions for what you expect to accomplish from the event.

What is your goal for this event? Is it to meet new potential clients? Is it to connect and collaborate with like-minded business owners? Is it to connect with people planning speaking events that you would be interested in attending? Be clear about why you are going.

When you attend the event, consider the venue. Is it a professional business? Is it a function hall? Is it a fun venue like a bowling alley or arcade? Is there a theme for the event?

The venue matters. If you go into a professional business event, where everyone is acting their most professional self, and you go in ready to have fun, it is automatic that your energy and their energy is not going to match, and you will likely not have a good time or make any lasting connections.

Energy flows in ripples everywhere all the time from everyone.

When you get to your event, before you go in, assess the energy. Stop for a moment. Be present and aware. Pay attention to anything your inner GPS may be saying to you. Is there a weird vibe coming from the venue? Is there an "air of excitement" around the venue?

Your inner GPS senses things long before your brain has a chance catch up. When you pay attention, you can use this valuable information to your advantage.

Upon entering the venue, what do you feel? Do you feel like you want to run back out? Do you feel like you need to proceed with caution? Do you feel like you want to jump right into the group and start connecting?

Your personal energy ripples out to others the moment you enter the room. You may find that as soon as you enter, you automatically lock eyes with a person across the room. You don't even know them yet and you feel like you "resonate" with them. That is their energy vibrating on the same frequency as yours. That person is likely going to be a great connection for you.

> *"Your inner thoughts aren't truly hidden.*
> *Their essence reflects in your energy.*
> *Energy speaks what you don't."*
> DRISHTI BABLANI

When you are aware of the energy around you, you also know when there is someone who is showing up with a mask on — not being their authentic self, so you know to proceed with caution.

The energy ripples you send out connect with the energy from everything and everyone around you.

Energy doesn't lie.

Finding and connecting with the right people is the key to business and life.

Understanding the energy behind these connections can help you not only create a more profitable business; it can also help you create better relationships with your friends and family.

As a business and mindset consultant, I help women business owners shift their mindset and energy to create a more profitable business and more enjoyable life.

Let's face it, being a business owner can get a bit overwhelming at times. When you learn how to master energy and mindset, business becomes easy and effortless allowing you to create a lifestyle business that you love.

Check out my free masterclass **"The 3 Most Important Mindset Shifts Most Business Owners Fail to Make"** at www.yourlifestylebusinessnow.com. It will help you begin to understand the power of your energy today."

The best way to connect with me is by joining our community on Facebook:

https://www.facebook.com/groups/womenoverwhelmed-tooverjoyed

When you learn how to harness the power of your energy and master your mindset, everything in life becomes easy and effortless.

CONNECT WITH ME: https://linktr.ee/reginaandler

STELLA HOH

I love to dedicate this chapter to my beautiful client family members. Without you, I would not be on this journey. You know who you are!

To my many mentors especially Terri Levine, Joel Bauer, and Peng Joon. Thanks for guiding the way.

Of course, to my family, especially to Daniel and my three gorgeous children who motivated me to be your model of excellence to create an impact in others' lives.

You are all the driving force for the work I am doing now.

Living my purpose and designing a legacy.

In love and gratitude, to you - Stella Hoh

HOW TO CREATE A RADICALLY SUCCESSFUL AND PROFITABLE BUSINESS

by Stella Hoh

THE JOURNEY TO SUCCESS

"Stella, I never had this kind of money ever! In my life."

I smiled.

ONE YEAR AGO...

"Stella, I have no more money left. This pandemic has literally stopped my commercial furniture design business, there are no more orders. And I have lost my income source. I am living in my office right now to save on my resources. I have to apply for government support as I don't know how long this pandemic is going to last. I'm angry, I'm frustrated with my current situation, and yet I do not know how to help myself. I am stuck. I don't know how to move on with my life and I can't live my life with dignity, have the income to support my own retirement, and live my own passion and purpose to help others."

My heart broke when I heard this.

This was the situation Joyce Pellegrini was in at that time. When the Covid pandemic hit in 2020, I had this inner calling in my heart that Joyce needed help. I reached out to her on Facebook Messenger. Invited her to one of my programs that I literally gave away during the pandemic. She was thrilled.

When we spoke on zoom, she finally shared her predicament. It shocked me. Although the pandemic made many lose their jobs, their business, and their families, this was particularly shocking as this was not the Joyce I knew. I came to know Joyce in 2019 on a cruise holiday/training with a mentor that we had in common. Joyce was self-driven, highly motivated, disciplined, and organized with an amazing energy of joy that was infectious. I could never have imagined her in this state. My heart literally broke. I knew that I wanted and had to help her.

During the cruise in 2019, she experienced a process that I helped her with. And she discovered that she had a fear of rejection from a four-year-old trauma. She felt rejected by her father. Deep inside me, I knew that would have impacted her money blocks as well as her wealth. We did a process, and when she got home, she sent me a video sharing that she achieved USD$10,000 sales in six days after that cruise.

Fast forward to the call during the pandemic when she lost her livelihood. Joyce was concerned she could not raise the money for the group mentorship program that she asked me for. However, she was willing to find a way to get her way forward in life so, she found the first deposit sum to begin a mentorship journey, my proven proprietary "**MindsetToProfits**" system, to work on pivoting online. She joined the journey in 2021.

She started making progress, and I strategized to help her build the first online business selling 200-plus bandanas that she made during the Covid-19 lockdown. She also landed her first order for her furniture business reconnecting with her client list. In no time, she was building her dream of 18 years in holistic healing both online and offline. In one weekend, she generated USD$25,000 in sales and has clients till February 2022. Her progress from being depressed to her success warmed my heart.

This is what mattered most to me.

Joyce told me she never had this kind of income, especially doing what she loved. She even had SBA loans offered to her. Joyce now has the money to retire, emotional freedom, and her own time to do what she loves, and she continues to save lives by reducing inflammation in the lives of her clients. She has achieved six figures in eight months with her determination, as well as accountability, community, mastermind training, and support through the "**MindsetToProfits**" program. She has since created more programs to impact lives and has similar dreams and alignment with why I do what I do - to impact lives.

However, if she didn't take a leap of faith in 2021 to invest in her business and mindset mentorship, she would not have achieved the freedom that she has now.

I'm grateful. Truly appreciate the trust that she has given me. Leveraging on my system, the platform I built supports her, helps her, and gives her the strength, accountability, and community, to work on growing and evolving her businesses as well as her inner self. In this journey, she also discovered that her fear of rejection from a 4-year-old trauma was one major block from wealth, confidence, self-esteem, and progress. She feared being rejected. With the additional mindset program "**Fearto-Power**" she has now unleashed all these subconscious blocks and achieved her success more swiftly and has fully embraced a gentler persona. She was able to connect to herself and her clients more effectively with credibility and visibility through heart-to-heart connection.

I WAS STUCK IN MY OWN WAYS!

I was in the real estate industry for more than 25 years. I worked in a multinational corporation, a real estate consultancy firm, as the head of investments, heading a 10-member team. We were transacting sales revenue to the tune of tens of billions over the years. I mentored the team from project inception, business development, marketing, closing, and negotiations.

However, one day I received a call. I was told that a team member, who just left for a better job, and became my client was found unconscious next to his car—dead. Cause of death: exhaustion. Derrick was pursuing his second master's, a national badminton player. I couldn't believe it. He was 38 years old, and I was two years younger than him. From that moment on, I knew that I didn't want to continue living as an ATM machine at the firm and dying at my work. I needed to live with a purpose. I wanted something more fulfilling.

I started attending personal development courses, signing up for seminars, meeting coaches, and mentors, and searching for my direction, and my purpose in life. I wanted to live a meaningful and beneficial life, impacting lives, and leaving a legacy in the hearts and minds of others.

I invested so much time and money. Are you like me? Lost, frustrated, and tired, searching for solutions, yet they didn't work.

One day, I had an AHA moment. I had started implementing and sharing the experience, skill sets, and knowledge I amassed over decades. I started gifting them, as my principle is to pay it forward.

Gift, and you shall be given (my personal quote).

THE BLUEPRINT

What if I can give you the blueprint that I used to start my coaching, and mentoring business from scratch? Yet, with my process, within a matter of months, my clients make their six figures, some built their new businesses with clear business strategies and earned their first four and five figures.

PILLAR 1: MINDSET

Fears stop one from pursuing their dreams. Joyce Pellegrini was fearful of rejection. She found out through one of my proprietary methods that her fear of rejection came from her 4-year-old trauma from her dad. She felt Dad rejected her, hence, she was in her own way with her fear of rejection. After walking through memory lane and letting go of this imprinted memory, she started to make cold calls for her furniture business and, in a few days, made her first ten thousand. Soon, we started working on her dream coaching business to help people to heal from their inflammation in the body with biofeedback.

The purpose is what drives business. A well-designed dream board focusing on contributing back would help manifest your dream faster. The universe has a way of rewarding those who focus on contributing back to the world. So, this dream board encompasses personal, family, wealth, and life pursuits as well as a contribution you would like to focus on. Whether it is a donation, charity, contributing with service or money, etc.

A long-term plan of 5-10 years and a short-term plan of 1-3 years would suffice due to the continuous fast-changing market.

Design your daily mantras, set intentions for your daily life, and work on what's working and not working yet.

Start implementing and changing how you design your life. The mistake many entrepreneurs make is they design their business first and end up working their life around it. Successful entrepreneurs design their life first and work their businesses around them to create impact and legacy.

PILLAR 2: MARKETING

In business, many entrepreneurs focus on their zone of genius, what they are good at. However, the oxygen for any business is MARKETING.

Remember, people buy mostly based on emotions. Have you gone shopping with the intention to buy an item and end up with a bag of non-necessities?

Having the right message to market helps one get the attention of your client. Know the pain of your client and explain how you bring them to paradise emotionally. Have clarity on the problem that you can help them solve and that will attract them to choose you as the logical choice to help them achieve what they desire.

Visit your customer's journey, and design one that takes care of what your client wants, not what you want for them.

PILLAR 3: MONETIZE

Leveraging social media is crucial in this current climate as paying for Facebook ads, google ads, YouTube ads, etc. can be so painfully expensive!

Focus on building credibility and visibility with social media. Showing your true authentic self and what your values are. Gifting training and resources through Facebook groups, Facebook lives, and even in free workshops. Building heart-to-heart connections and relationships help draw clients who resonate with your values and energy. Do this and they will choose you as their mentor or coach.

Lead generation

Start building leads. This means new prospects, using social media and landing pages, by giving away free gifts with real value!

Have your clear headline and sub-headline directed at your audience with the problem you can solve to achieve the outcome they desire.

Nurturing leads

Create automated systems to connect with your leads. Nurture cold leads to warm and hot leads who will raise their hands to choose you as their mentor or coach. Reactivating old clients and gaining new clients through an automated simple technical system allows you more time freedom instead of sitting at your computer sending emails and putting out content on social media.

What if it is so simple, to build your business systems and process without complicated tech? All it takes is implementation, being accountable for your process, and having a heart connection to build real relationships with your clients.

HOW TO LEARN MORE?

If you want to achieve success for your coaching and consulting business, connect with me and I would love to gift you the resources and free training.

Happy to serve you.

With Love & Gratitude

Watch this free training

www.SecretForBusinessSuccess.com

Connect with me for a breakthrough call at

https://www.stellahoh.com/breakthrough

https://linktr.ee/stellahoh

VAL BULLERMAN

To my husband, kids, and grandkids, my love connections that make me joyful and rich in many ways!

CONNECT AND GROW RICH

by Val Bullerman

I started my business like many entrepreneurs, looking for guidance on how to grow my business. Knowing I needed clients, but not sure exactly how to do that on a consistent basis. I got my website and business cards ~ ready for business. I waited and I waited. I am a really good coach, where are the people? They were not lining up outside my door. If something did not change, I'd have to get a J.O.B.

I purchased a couple of "how to get clients" programs, but they either felt too pushy or too salesy. I knew that I had to have a process that would allow me to feel authentic about offering my services and others felt good buying them.

So, I created the Connect and Grow Rich system. Within a couple of months, I had 14 clients! My Connection Philosophy also took me from Iowa to Amsterdam and around the world. For 3 years, I traveled to the Netherlands to host and speak at events, retreats, and classes. In today's world, you do not even have to travel, unless you are like me and love travel. Connection has truly given me the ability to create my very own ripple effect and become a worldwide, award-winning speaker and business coach.

While connection is at the core of my success, it did not always and sometimes still doesn't come easily. When not on stage, coaching, or teaching, I tend to be a quiet person. I love to observe others and learn what makes them tick. After an event or travel, I need recharge time. I love connection and I love my quiet time also. Whether you are an introvert or extrovert, this system will allow you to connect with less effort and be more effective in creating relationships.

Using the *Connect and Grow Rich* system, I am able to create and teach how to make 6 figures in a year, in a month, and even in one day. Using this system, I often have people asking me, so how can I work with you BEFORE I get to the offer!

I am going to share with you the strategies and mindsets I used to create a "wildly" successful business and a life I love.

THE CONNECTION PHILOSOPHY

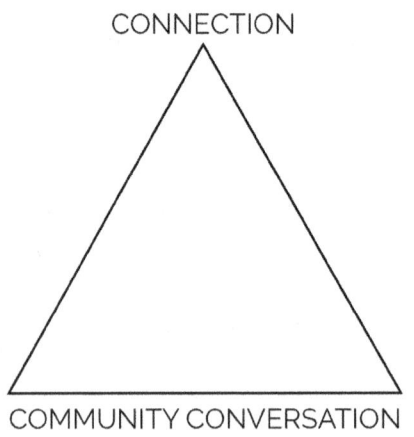

CONNECTION

COMMUNITY CONVERSATION

CONNECTION is an interesting word. I like to think of it as developing a deep bond with someone and they feel seen and valued. When someone feels connected to you, and you to them, it feels like coming home when you spend time with them. This also applies to having a connection with yourself. If you do not feel a connection with yourself, it is more challenging to connect with others. Be sure to take some time for you to know who you are and what you want to do. Be clear and loving. Stay away from criticisms and acknowledge how far you have come.

CREATING COMMUNITY and knowing who your community is will take the guesswork out of what to say and where are the people you are meant to connect with. You do not have to have a huge community to create success, you have to be clear about who your community is. They are waiting for you.

The final step is CONVERSATION. This is the step people most fear. It is also the step that can be the easiest once you've done a few. The art of connection is all about the conversation.

Ok, let's put the **Connection Philosophy** to work.

When communicating with clients and potential clients there are different levels of connection. The highest level is to have someone in person, in front of you having a conversation. One of the lowest levels of connection in your business is to be behind your computer, tweaking your website, surfing Facebook, and sending messages. I'm not saying to never send messages. And when sending messages, be sure to keep it in mind to add some extra connection with your words.

I have created a **Connection Scale** for my clients. Kind of like a connection thermometer. The difference in creating a relationship that is long-lasting is based on the level of connection you have with them. As my gift to you, I'm sharing this tool with you, so you have it to refer to and get some great ideas on how to create more connections in your world. You will find it in my Facebook Group: **facebook.com/groups/ValsBusinessSuccessGroup**

Choose the 2 that you feel will enhance your connections and put them into action. Notice how it gets easier the more you allow for the connections.

So, you know what you want to sell. You know people want it. (If you don't – stop reading right now and email me to get clarity around your tribe and what you want to offer them)

Where do those people who want it hang out? You have to go where they are – not expect them to come to you. So, find a networking group, live or online event where you will find your client or customer. You might have to visit different ones at first.

I'll use a client case study to walk you through this process. Caroline came to me after being in business for a couple of years and was making just under 6 figures. She belonged to some networking groups, but she had not yet gotten any business and was ready to quit all of them. I asked her to not quit them for 2 months and let's do some things differently, so she could get different results. She agreed.

The first thing we did was determine how many clients she wanted to have a full practice. She wanted 10 clients. She currently had 2.

At each of the networking groups/events, she networked in a way different than before. She engaged people by asking questions about them and their businesses. She used the 80 / 20 rule – she talked only 20% of the time and allowed the other person to talk 80% of the time. She didn't even share what she did unless they asked and then it was a quick "lean in" marketing message. A "lean in" marketing message is one that when you say it, people lean forward and either ask for more information

or say, "Oh my gosh, do I need you" or "I have a friend who is in need of your services!"

As she worked her way around the room, she asked for business cards of those that were good connections for her. A good connection is someone that either is a center of influence or possible clients or a possible connection for speaking or other partnerships. On average she got 3 to 5 possible connections.

On the back of the cards, she wrote a quick note about the person she met. It might be a business note or a personal note. Something that would help identify them to her.

Caroline did this everywhere she went in her community: at the Chamber of Commerce events, at other events that she attended, and in networking groups. Your community is much bigger than just networking groups.

Caroline has jumped past 6 figures to $200,000 using this system. Today, she doesn't have to work this system each week, she integrates it as she moves through her month connecting with the right people wherever she goes.

Special note about events—you are only gathering cards at the events, you are not selling or even sharing a lot about what you do. You are at someone else's event and the attendees belong to the event leader until they leave. Once they leave the event when it's over, you can follow up with them.

It doesn't matter if your community is local, nationwide, or worldwide. Connecting is what makes the world go round— both in business and your personal life.

Did you know you are networking everywhere you go? Note I didn't say selling everywhere you go, but that could be a result of really great networking.

I love connecting with my communities—local and worldwide. It's a core part of my business, and it also builds a great support network for me. My focus with groups is to connect. Not to connect with every single person on a deep level, but to really connect with those that I feel that connection with.

One of the things about networking that makes me giggle is the person that is handing out their card to everyone in the room as if they are dealing with them. Why? Because you and I know what happens to those cards. They either end up in a pile or file on your desk or in the wastebasket.

It is more important for you to get the cards of those you've made a good connection with—it doesn't really matter if you give them your card or not. Yes, I said it. It really doesn't matter if they get your card. Why? Because you are going to follow up right away with them while they still remember you.

Create connections with those who feel like you could have a bond or has possibilities. I normally set a goal for 3 to 5 of those cards. You can get more, but having a system in place for what to do with them is critical. Otherwise, you've just wasted your time.

Now comes the fun part. When Caroline got home, it was time to set up the connections.

I taught her to take a blank piece of paper and at the top, write the date and the event name. Then tape the cards down the left-hand side. Next to each card she wrote the event name and date, notes she remembered, whatever was on the back of the card. (You can set it up on a word doc too, but this works fine.)

At this point, you can do one of two things, you can start calling those you met and have an informal conversation....the structure for that is next. Or you can send an email asking to set up a time for the two of you to chat. You can try both ways.

Normally I'd recommend the phone call, but in this instance, an email with a link (like Time Trade or other scheduling programs). I'm happy to share my follow-up email in my Facebook group: **facebook.com/groups/ValsBusinessSuccessGroup**.

I get over 90% positive responses with this email. Part of that high response rate is that these messages are sent the very next day so I am fresh in their minds.

So, you will set up a 30-minute conversation with that person. I also do these in person if possible. I set aside Wednesday mornings and meet at a coffee shop.

The next step is the connection meeting – in person or on the phone, they run about the same. Your intention in this meeting is NOT to share everything you do.

Your intention is to interview them like a rock star. Asking them lots of questions about why they got into their business, who is the leading expert in their field, and finding out who they are as a person.

Again, the 80/20 rule is in effect. They are talking 80% or the time and you are talking 20% or less. Sometimes at the end of these connection meetings, people will say "This has been one of the best conversations I've had in a long time." I smile and agree. They feel like they have been heard; and what a gift that is!

At the end of this conversation, you should have a great idea of what their needs are and who they are as a person. If it's appropriate, you can invite them to a conversation with you about what you do.

A lot of times, the conversation would sound like this:

Them: Boy, I have really enjoyed talking with you, Val.

Me: Yes, me too!

Them: But wait, I haven't heard anything about your business.

Me: Oh, that's ok. In fact, what I'd like to do is give you an experience of what I do. I offer a free session called "Boost your Business" Together, we'll look at what's happening in your business and where you might be stuck. How does that sound?

Them: That would be great!

We set the appointment right there.

I never had anyone say no to this offer using this technique.

The focus of this connection meeting is just that...to connect. It's not that you can't share anything about you as a person, but the focus is on them....remember, they are the rock star. Who wouldn't want to be treated like a rock star??

You can tweak this conversation in lots of ways—if you are a health coach, your session could be "A Healthier, Wealthier You". Together, you'll look at where they are in their health journey and see how the connection to how your health affects your wealth.

This is just an example, but you get the idea. You just have to have a session to offer them. Make sure the name is enticing to them.

A quick word of caution here. In the connection meeting, as a business coach, I would not ask about how their business is doing in depth. When they go there, I steer them on to another topic. A health coach wouldn't do their connection meeting asking all about the person's health. The other person will feel a "salesy" pitch coming. Instead, you drive the conversation so you get to know them as a person and whatever they want to share. You will purposefully point them away from the obvious subject you might sell them on.

So now you are establishing community and creating connections. It's time for the CONVERSATION. Now that you've developed the know, like, and trust factor, it's time to have a conversation that might result in a sale, or a referral or a new resource. Breathe deep, here we go.

This is when people freeze up and say, "I don't want to sell anyone. I don't want them to feel bad. I just want to connect with everyone." These are all excellent excuses to stay stuck! AND broke!

A sales conversation is all about the give. You are offering them the gift of your service. Don't be selfish and keep your gift to yourself! Change will not happen for that other person unless they buy, and sometimes they need to buy big for a big transformation. The quicker you start believing that or something close, the faster you will grow your business.

Practice will help you get good at having these conversations in an effective way. I'm going to share my outline of how I conduct my conversations. You can find it in my Business Success Group Facebook Group: **facebook.com/groups/ValsBusinessSuccessGroup**.

Please note that I do hold these in a way that feels like a conversation instead of me "selling" something right off the bat. The selling is happening during each step, but the sale is only them deciding yes or no. It's that simple.

While I can't teach the entire training on having this conversation, there are a few important points I want to share with you.

This is a give-and-take conversation. They are still talking the majority of the time. While you are in control of where the conversation is going, they are feeling heard and getting lots of clarity and insight into what's really going on in their business. Emotions may come up, including frustration, tears, and anger. This is just a part of their process.

Keep in mind, you are not selling your process. You are selling the result they've asked you to help them with.

Most people shy away from the urgency, and this is where people need the most help to realize what will happen if they don't get this fixed. This is where the real magic can happen for your potential client. It is working with the gap—where they are and where they want to be. This can be uncomfortable. It's up to you to become comfortable with that tension. Do not try to relieve the tension by making them feel better. That tension is what could save their business or their life.

It could be the difference between them getting what they want from the business or not and having to get a job, die an early death, or ruin a relationship. I'm not being dramatic; they won't make the big transformation they want without making a purchase with you. You can't help them if they don't buy. It is all about you serving them.

During the close, I want you to imagine yourself coming around alongside of them and helping them to make a yes or no decision. It's that simple. They will have excuses come up, but it's just their fear stuff. Remind them of their urgency—what will happen if they don't fix this? Instead of being head-to-head, energetically come alongside them to help them see the reality.

This conversation should take about 30 minutes on average. One word of caution. Fight the urge to coach or perform your service during this conversation. This is not the time for a band-aid to their problem. It's time for them to make a concrete move towards a solution to their problem. The definition and clarity that comes from this conversation are full of value —more value at this moment than you trying to give them a quick solution.

This truly has been the special sauce for my business and can be adapted for yours. It moved my business forward quickly when I first started and I still use this process today. I love connecting and building community. I love conversations that serve up opportunities for all.

Connection is a critical component of life and business.

I would love it if you would connect with me in our Facebook Group—*Val's Business Success Group* for some tools to make running your business easier and some really great conversations. You can go here:

facebook.com/groups/ValsBusinessSuccessGroup

www.ingramcontent.com/pod-product-compliance
Lightning Source LLC
Chambersburg PA
CBHW070716130626
46553CB00005B/2008